Walt Disney World
Peak Seasons

Walt Disney World Peak Seasons

✦

Maximizing your Disney Vacation

Scott Donahue

iUniverse, Inc.
New York Lincoln Shanghai

Walt Disney World Peak Seasons
Maximizing your Disney Vacation

iUniverse books may be ordered through booksellers or by contacting:

iUniverse
2021 Pine Lake Road, Suite 100
Lincoln, NE 68512
www.iuniverse.com
1-800-Authors (1-800-288-4677)

ISBN: 978-0-595-47727-2 (pbk)
ISBN: 978-0-595-91990-1 (ebk)

Printed in the United States of America

For Becky, Jacey, and Peyton, may all your wishes come true.

Becky, your support has meant so much to me I cannot explain it in words. Each day you have believed in me and continued to provide me with the motivation needed to accomplish anything I put my mind toward. I love you and appreciate everything you do.

Jacey, you probably don't realize it, but you have given me so much support by always asking about my book and showing me that it is ok to try something, even if success doesn't come right away. I find inspiration in you by how successful you are. You work so hard in everything you do, and you have shown me that hard work can pay off.

Peyton, ever since the day you were born, I knew you were something special. You have had to live with Adult Polycystic Kidney Disease all your life. You are only eight years old and have been taking medicines since you were a few days old. Never once have you complained about having to take them. You try your best in everything you do even though the disease limits many activities for you. You are my inspiration! The way in which you display strength in your young life shows me that anything is possible.

This book is about taking a chance, having the courage to take a risk, and most importantly to show others that you can make your dreams come true, all you need is a little courage.

"Any wish is possible.
All it takes is a little courage to set it free"

—Jiminy Cricket

Contents

About the Author

Scott Donahue is a middle school teacher and coach. He has a Bachelor of Science degree from Illinois State University and a Masters degree in Health, Physical Education, and Recreation from Emporia State University.

After eight years of teaching 10-14 year olds, he decided a vacation was a must. In 2003 Scott, his wife Becky (also a teacher) and daughters Jacey and Peyton packed the van and headed south. It only took one trip and the whole family was hooked on all things Disney.

Since that initial vacation Scott and his family have taken thirteen trips, all during the summer, Spring Break, or the Christmas season. He truly is an expert in maximizing the fun despite the crowds. Friends and family alike have benefitted from Scott's words of wisdom when planning a trip to Walt Disney World. Scott and his family reside in Peoria, Illinois.

Acknowledgements

I would like to thank my wife, Becky, for all her help, support, and belief that I could create something like this book. I also want to thank my family for all their support in this process as well. My two daughters, Jacey and Peyton, have provided me with so much inspiration and courage to take a risk and believe in myself.

When I first started to write down comments after each trip, I never dreamed that a book would come of it. As I began to write little notes about our vacations (what worked and what didn't), reading the endless Disney guide books, and taking thirteen trips since 2003, it made me realize that I had something to offer people who vacation at Walt Disney World during the peak seasons.

So with the support of my family, I decided to give writing a book a try. My wife's patience and confidence in me cannot be described in words. Without her help, none of this would have been possible. I am a believer in all that Disney stands for. It has provided our family with memories that will last a lifetime.

I want to thank all of you fellow Disney lovers that have helped with and have visited my website (http://www.wdwpeakseasons.com). I created the website as a way to give many Disney fans a place where they could get the information they needed in a timely manner. The website is now serving as a compliment to the book and will hopefully continue to evolve and improve.

Finally, I want to thank all of the Cast Members at Walt Disney World. You are the ones who make our trips memorable. You make every guest feel like he or she is the most important person in the world. Your dedication and belief in Disney is what makes it such a magical place.

Preface

Walt Disney World is the number one family vacation destination in the world. Crowds flock to sunny Florida to soak up the rays and, with luck, a bit of pixie dust. Along with countless others, my family journeyed to this magical world with visions of Mickey and Minnie, a castle with real princesses, and rides that went beyond our imaginations. We waited excitedly for the big day when we would pass through the lands that promised us fantasy, the future, and adventure around every turn. What we found, however, was more of a world the Disney villains might have Imagineered. We encountered tremendous crowds, cranky parents, whining kids, enormous groups of teenagers, and more terrors than any tower could have caused. What we found were … the Peak Seasons.

Had this book been available in 2003, when my family made our first trek into Mickey's home turf, perhaps I would have been prepared. Sure I had done some research at the local bookstore, but none of those guides truly captured the reality of a peak season. I never realized that the summer months are, for lack of a better term, crazy! However, somehow we still had fun even as we jostled our way through the stroller brigade, the blazing Florida heat, the "Johnny come lately" parade cutters, and resort pools so crowded we had to squeeze our way into the water.

Once we returned home and perused our 300 plus photos, we decided that we just had to go back, and soon. We weren't sure if Santa could make the trip so we decided Spring Break would fit wonderfully into our schedule as teachers. My wife and I agreed that Walt Disney World would be a great retreat from our hectic daily lives in the middle school. Once we walked onto Main Street U.S.A. we had to wonder if we left the school hallways at all. If we thought summer was a peak season, Spring Break really was "A Whole New World."

Imagine if you will, every high school student from around the country going on a field trip to the same place at the same exact time. That's pretty much what we encountered. We thought from the knowledge we gained on our summer trip, along with additional research in our travel books, we were ready to handle any challenge that came our way. Not so much. We had heard of elevated crowds. Have you ever been to Tomorrowland at night during Spring Break? The jaws-of-life would have come in handy in our attempt to make our way to Fantasyland. Back at the resort, I understood we were lacking in the way of peak season preparation. Something had to be done.

Before I could be completely convinced that our teacher/school schedule coincided with the busiest times at Walt Disney World, I decided we needed one more research vacation. We took on the granddaddy of them all—Christmas week. We left Santa some Mickey Ears, packed our bags, and headed south. BAM! It was like a castle wall jumping out of thin air. Our vacation came to a screeching halt as we found ourselves in the midst of another peak season. I knew then that these peak seasons were different. We needed a way to help others enjoy a vacation when the crowds are at a maximum.

In <u>Walt Disney World Peak Seasons: Maximizing your Disney Vacation</u>, I lay out these details. I want you to truly understand that although the parks may be at capacity, there is a way to maximize your vacation with very little headache. I will help you when you have to make the trip during the summer, Spring Break, or the Christmas season because of school schedules. Not everyone can pull their children out of school to go during the "off-season." In a perfect world, we would go during January or September. Life isn't perfect, and we have to go with what fits our daily lives. To us, and thousands of other families, that is a peak season.

Other tour books may devote a page or two to the summer or holiday seasons. These time frames are my main focus. My methods are quite different as well. I haven't sent a hired staff into the parks to get information. We pack up the van, drive seventeen hours from Peoria, Illinois, and tour the parks with two young girls. I really do have a Disney Peak Season Family. With thirteen family trips to Walt Disney World under my belt since 2003, all during the summer, late December, and Spring Break, I have the knowledge and expertise to give you what you want when it comes to planning a peak season trip—the truth. The peak seasons may be intimidating, but I am living proof that it is possible to have a magical vacation despite the crowds.

Introduction

Walt Disney World. Those three little words can bring a smile to a child's face in an instant. The thought of visiting Mickey and the gang can set a youngster into a fit of excited giggles. A child may imagine a place where princesses rule and fairies sprinkle pixie dust. Pirates and villains may inhabit the land. Whatever the dream, a child knows that Walt Disney World is a magical place. Grown-ups too may picture a leisurely stroll on Main Street USA, a quiet walk through Fantasyland, or a heart racing trip through a mountain. Dreams can come true for Disney visitors of any age. Planning a dream vacation to this special place requires more than the average trip to the beach or nearest amusement park. That's where <u>Walt Disney World Peak Seasons: Maximizing your Disney Vacation</u> comes into play. Sure you can "play it by ear" when you get to the parks. Sure you can "make it up as you go." However, if you want to maximize your time and still experience the magic that Disney has to offer, a game plan is a must.

First of all, the time of year that you schedule your trip is a major decision. Throughout the year crowds, special events, and even park maintenance will vary. For many of us, the peak seasons are the only time available to vacation at Walt Disney World. So the real question is…. what are the peak seasons? The peak seasons are defined as the times of the year when the majority of travelers venture to Walt Disney World to vacation. The peak seasons can be broken down into three separate times of the year: Spring Break, summer, and Christmas. Each of these seasons provides a different and unique experience at Walt Disney World. What is the one constant during each of these times of the year? The parks are more crowded than at any time. The reason they are packed is obvious … there is no school. Most schools throughout the country generally have some time off for Spring Break, summer, and Christmas. Even schools in other countries may have holiday time where the students can travel. Many people are not able to take their children out of school to go on vacation. Their only other alternative is to wait until school goes on a break or vacation. Thus Spring Break, summer, and Christmas provide a fantastic opportunity to go to Walt Disney World. For many of us, this is all we know. A park where you can walk down Main Street U.S.A. without being bumped around, maneuvering through

85,000 plus of your newest friends, or looking up at wait times for E-ticket attractions at a minimum of 120 minutes would seem foreign to us.

Who, what, when, where, why, and how always seem to be brought up when traveling during the peak seasons. Who goes to Walt Disney World during peak seasons? What kind of weather will I have? When should I make my reservations? Why do I have to plan so far in advance? Why is everyone here? How packed are the resorts? How packed are the parks? How long are waits for the E-Ticket rides? We will attempt to answer these questions and throw in a little extra magic along the way.

1

Peak Seasons—What are they?

Spring Break

Let's focus on Spring Break first. This is the time anywhere from Mid-February to the week after Easter. Who goes to Walt Disney World during this time? It seems like everyone! Walt Disney World is a perfect destination for those of us who are from up North and need a warmer vacation to help recover from the long winter. Many people throughout the country can travel during this time because most schools offer a week or so of vacation time. With the kids out of school, it marks the opportune time to head to Walt Disney World. What kind of weather will you have? This will vary, but tempratures in the day are in the 70's and evenings in the 50's. There is usually very little rain during this time frame. This is one of the more pleasant things about traveling during this time. Most days you can be comfortable wearing shorts and a light jacket in the morning, a t-shirt and shorts throughout the day, then maybe a jacket or sweatshirt at night, if needed.

When should you make your reservations? Hopefully, you have called Walt Disney World many months in advance to book your resort and room type. This is imperative because during Spring Break rooms and some resorts fill up a few months in advance. Usually traveling during this time Disney offers few discounts because they do not need to. The rooms will be full regardless. Plan accordingly and pay close attention to the rack rate listed on the Walt Disney World Web site.

Why do you have to plan so far in advance? Again, you are traveling during a peak season, so it will be one of the most crowded of times at Walt Disney World. There can be in upwards of 250,000 people at all four parks and resorts during peak seasons. Those who get the jump on everyone else get the best dining reservations, room views, and resorts they want. Those who procrastinate will have to settle with what is left.

Why is everyone here? Walt Disney World is a safe environment. It is a place where kids and adults can be comfortable and know that it will be an enjoyable vacation. There is something about being at Walt Disney World that takes us to a place where we can forget about the troubles that we have in our everyday lives. It allows all our problems to be left behind, even if it is only for a few days. There are few places in the world that can offer that and present something for every age group, as well.

How packed are the parks and resorts? There can be in the neighborhood of 250,000 people on the Walt Disney World property during a peak season. We have seen the parks on certain days close to the public because they are at capacity. Since we are talking about Spring Break, Easter Sunday is the one day that Magic Kingdom will fill to capacity by about 11:00 AM. Unofficially, Magic Kingdom has a capacity of about 95,000 people. The resorts will be packed to capacity as well. Many times there will be zero rooms available on property if you wait until the last minute.

How long are the wait times for the E-Ticket rides? Well, let's assume you ignore everything we have laid out in the book, you do not utilize FASTPASS, and you do not arrive at park opening. The E-Ticket rides during Spring Break can have wait times of 120-240 minutes, depending on the ride and the time of day. This is why if you are traveling during the peak seasons it is a must to get to the parks early and use FASTPASS.

A side note is that many times during Spring Break, the morning Extra Magic Hours (EMH) for Magic Kingdom will be at 7:00 AM. Yes, I know that is incredibly early, and it is going to be tough to get the kids out of bed as well as leave the resort by 6:20 AM or so. If you get to bed early the night before and plan your Mickey wake-up call for the crack of dawn, you can literally get most things in Magic Kingdom done by noon and still have a relaxing afternoon. It is actually a pretty neat experience to see the sun rise while walking on Main Street U.S.A. Believe me, it is well worth it.

WDW Peak Season Advice

Do:

- Get to the parks early

- Plan on it being cool in the morning and evenings, but very comfortable during the day

- Take a break in mid-afternoon

- Utilize FASTPASS

- Utilize EMH's in the morning

Don't:

- Think you will just walk onto any rides you want

- Stay all day in the parks. Go back to your resort for a break

- Plan on swimming every day. The temperatures vary so take it day by day

- Think you can eat at any sit down restaurant without making a reservation far in advance

Summer Season

This ranges from June through Mid August. This is usually the time again when school is out, and it allows parents to take their kids on vacation. This timeframe though is a bit less crowded than Spring Break or Winter Holidays. Why you ask? Well first off, it's HOT! Hades would be quite comfortable in the parks. Temperatures usually will hit the upper 90's with the Heat Index breaking 100 degrees Fahrenheit. For some it is just too hot to walk around the parks on vacation. Couple that with a high crowd count, and it can make for a less than thrilling vacation.

Secondly, many kids have activities in the summer such as Little League and softball so some families will opt to vacation during Spring Break or winter and by-pass summer. That way they do not disrupt the activities of their kids. Plus during the summer it is easier to go to a local swimming pool to stay refreshed.

Now a few points need to be made if you have to vacation during the summer. With it being so hot, there are some safety precautions you need to follow. First, stay hydrated. The Florida heat can get to the best of us, so drink plenty of fluids before, during, and after your day at the parks. It is a good idea to drink a bottle of water before you go, take that bottle into the parks with you and fill it up all day long. This will save you money, and you can even get ice for free from an outdoor stand that has ice. You can pay $2.00 per bottle of water throughout the day. Either way you need to continuously drink fluids. Don't wait until you are thirsty. That is the biggest mistake people make during the summer.

Next make sure you have plenty of sunscreen. Apply it every hour or so. The sun will be beating down on you and you do not want a sun burn to ruin your trip. A misting fan of some sort is also valuable. Just a quick spray or two may be enough to help you get through that long queue at Expedition Everest.

When you tour the parks in the summer again the idea is to beat the heat. To do this you will want to get to parks early and leave by afternoon when it becomes the hottest part of the day. Trust me, it will be unbearable in the afternoon. When all the late sleepers start arriving, you can wave goodbye to them as you leave the park and head back to your resort. Use the afternoon time to either relax in the room, or go take a dip in the pool. Keep in mind though that in the summer it tends to rain most afternoons around 3-6 PM so plan your swim accordingly. The rain will move on and as the sun begins to fade, you can return to the parks a bit fresher than everyone else and a lot less frustrated. You will realize how rejuvenated you truly are when you watch others getting off the bus tired, sweaty, cranky, and generally not feeling especially magical.

The next tip is something that people sometimes forget about, but it can make your day much more enjoyable. It pertains to your clothing. The key here is to wear items that will pull the moisture away from your body. You want to avoid cotton shirts. You will see person after person with sweat pouring through their shirts. These are the people who are wearing cotton shirts. Don't get us wrong, we all have to wear Mickey shirts while on vacation, just wear them at night when it is a tad cooler. For daytime touring of the parks you should have shirts that are made of polyester, which wicks moisture away from your body and helps cool you down. Most manufacturers have some form of this. These shirts are a must. Trust us it will make you much more comfortable throughout the day. As for shoes, just make sure you have something comfortable as you will be walking quite a bit and you don't want to get blisters. You will walk several miles throughout the day without ever realizing it.

Now that we have gotten you past the heat factor, there's just one more thing to discuss about the summer touring plan. This is winter in South America, which means only one thing.... tour groups! In some ways they have gotten a bad rap, but in general here is what you should look for. There are groups, usually all wearing the same colored shirts of about 20-50 teenagers, with an adult in front of them and another behind them each carrying a flag. They typically are from Brazil and many do not speak English which causes problems for some when trying to follow directions. As with any large group of 12-18 year olds, sometimes they are rude and cut in line and things like that, other times they follow the rules. Our advice is just to avoid them. In my experience, they rarely get to the parks at park opening (yet another reason to get there ASAP). If you are approaching a ride and see fifty of the same shirts lining up, just come back to that ride later. It may alter your touring plan a bit, but trust us, it will be worth it. Go on to another ride and remind yourself to come back to that ride later. By doing this you can usually avoid headaches caused by enormous lines. Parades are another thing all together. You should really only view parades if you have never seen them before. The reason being when you vacation during peak seasons everyone wants to see the parades and things can sometimes get heated. The summertime seems to be the worst because in the excitement the large tour groups may push their way in front of you or your family. Since the groups can be fifty or more, this can lead to frustration issues for you. If you see the tour groups coming close to your spot, it would be a good idea to just get up and move to another spot in the parade route. Again nothing necessarily against the tour groups, but sometimes it is just better to avoid any potential conflicts. If you can follow most of these suggestions your summer trip can be a very fun experience.

WDW Peak Season Advice

Do:

- Get to the park early

- Drink plenty of water

- Wear moisture wicking clothing to keep you cool

- Wear athletic type shoes

- Plan on leaving in early afternoon to go relax or swim

- Plan on it raining in the late afternoon

- Plan on clear skies when you return to the parks at night

- Avoid large Tour Groups if possible

Don't:

- Wait until you feel thirsty to drink

- Wear cotton shirts during the day

- Wear sandals or flip-flops

- Try to stay the entire day and not go back for a mid-afternoon break

- Forget your ponchos if it calls for rain in the morning

Christmas Holidays

First, let me say that in my opinion, this may be the most beautiful season to go to Walt Disney World. There are holiday decorations everywhere! The resorts, the Cast Members, and the characters are all spruced up for the season. Everything is decorated in holiday trimmings. Because of the decorations, this makes Walt Disney World a must-see for families. The World looks so much different than the rest of the year. Many schools throughout the country have Christmas break a few days before Christmas continuing until the first week in January. Walt Disney World becomes a preferred vacation destination at this time because many families are missing the warmth from the past summer and want to enjoy the holiday season. Thus Walt Disney World offers both sun and holiday magic. With an extended vacation, it marks the perfect opportunity for families to get away and spend time at Walt Disney World. Couple that with others who just want to experience Walt Disney World during the holiday season, and it sets up a near capacity vacation destination.

If your childrens' winter break begins about five to six days before Christmas, you may be in luck. From Christmas Day until New Years Day, Walt Disney World will be more crowded than any other time of the year, yes even Spring Break. If you can get to Walt Disney World a few days before Christmas day you will have a bit of an advantage. You will notice that as the days creep closer to Christmas day, the resorts as well as the parks will begin to slowly fill up. This is ok though. In our experience, if you tour using the same principles as Spring Break and summer you will be just fine. Get to the parks early! The exception here is the weather. It can range from highs in the 80's during the day to lows in the 40's on some nights. This makes swimming hit or miss each day. It all depends on if it is warm enough for you. On many winter trips I have seen lifeguards in jackets and pants while guests are splashing around in the water. You will probably want to pack some pants as well as shorts to wear. You might be able to get by with a light jacket and pants or even a sweatshirt and shorts. The wintertime weather varies so much it is hard to say exactly what to wear. The one good thing about traveling during winter is that you are not so hot that you need to get back to your resort to rest. This is one time your touring plan will differ from what I have previously said.

I still stand by the notion that you need to get to the parks at opening. Instead of leaving in the afternoon to get back to your resort to rest however, you may not need to. You probably won't be exhausted from the heat, so it may be better to use your time to tour some festivities around Walt Disney World. Instead of going back to your own resort, go visit other resorts. Each resort has holiday decorations to admire. Some even have holiday activities planned which may interest your children. My daughters have each created ornaments made from ostrich shells and have helped bake Christmas cookies. Ask at the resort's front desk. Sometimes people get so wrapped up in the parks during the holiday season they forget that each resort offers something unique as well. Be sure to see the incredible life-size gingerbread house at the Grand Floridian or the breathtaking tree at the Animal Kingdom Lodge. After an afternoon visit to another resort or two, you have your evenings open to enjoy one of the many nighttime activities inside the parks. You do need to be aware that most parks will offer something special in regards to holiday lights at night, so plan on visiting each park during the day as well as the evening. They appear to be two different parks with the lights off and on.

All in all, the Christmas holiday season is the one time of the year that you won't be too frustrated with the high crowds. The backdrop of decorations and lights offers such a warm and special feeling you will have a hard time believing you are in the middle of Florida during Christmas time.

Note: For traveling during any of the peak seasons, you must plan ahead if you want to eat at certain restaurants. You can call Disney 180 days in advance of your trip to make dining reservations. I know that it seems like there is no way you can plan 180 days in advance where you are going to want to eat, but trust us, these fill up fast during Spring Break and winter. You do have a better chance in the summer. We have seen many guests walk up to a restaurant's check-in during a peak season, and walk away disappointed after being told that the restaurant is full.

It is imperative that you research the different restaurants and their menus (there are various web sites that offer this information), and make your reservations as soon as you can.

WDW Peak Season Advice

Do:

- Get to the parks early

- Go visit other resorts to view their holiday decorations

- Take time to enjoy the various holiday activities

- Realize that the temperatures will vary greatly

- Visit each park during the daytime and the nighttime at least once

Don't:

- Think you will be able to swim everyday

- Think you will be able to walk onto rides

- Think that you will be able to get your choice of resort or restaurant if you wait until the last minute

2

What to know before you go

This cannot be stressed enough, plan before you go. If you are traveling to Walt Disney World at a time when school is out, do not wait until a month before your trip to Walt Disney World to start your preparation. It is a must to begin the process at least 3-6 months in advance. Many people make the mistake of thinking that they will be able to walk right into the parks, walk onto every ride with minimum wait time, get the resort they want, and get into any restaurant to eat any day or time. If you are vacationing during the peak seasons (Spring Break, summer, and Christmas) this strategy will not work, and you may be very disappointed.

What should you know before you go? You should plan, plan, and plan. There are several factors that you must consider before you go, the first being the weather. Orlando weather in general provides a great climate most of the year. The exceptions are in the summer months, when come mid-afternoon you will most likely need to find air conditioning as a way to refresh yourself and cool down. The summer months also supply the most rainfall. It seems that every day during the summer you can expect an afternoon shower or thunderstorm. Listed below are the average temperatures for Orlando as well as rainfall per month.

*During the winter months you will have to dress warmly (sweatshirt and pants) in the mornings and evenings, and peel away a layer as the temperatures rise throughout the day.

Month	High	Low	Rainfall
January	72	50	2.4"
February	74	51	2.4"
March	79	56	3.5"
April	83	60	2.4"

May	88	66	3.7"
June	91	71	7.3"
July	92	73	7.3"
August	92	73	6.4"
September	90	72	6.2"
October	85	66	3.4"
November	79	59	2.5"
December	73	53	2.3"

Now that you have an idea about the weather you will encounter, a good tip for packing would be to pack for the coldest temperatures as you can always take layers off. One big mistake that many tourists make is thinking Orlando is warm all year long and all hours of the day and night. We have seen many visitors show up at the parks wearing a t-shirt and shorts in December because they did not pack any warm clothes. They are left to shiver and freeze until it warms up or spend $40 on a sweatshirt.

Walt Disney World also has different crowd patterns each day. Historically each park has more visitors on certain days of the week. The reason for this varies for everyone. Many times people will arrive at Walt Disney World on a Sunday and the first park they choose is the most famous, Magic Kingdom. Thus Monday is a busy day for that park. A park may have Extra Magic Hours (EMH) on a certain day of the week all year and that may factor in as well. Does that mean that every Monday the Magic Kingdom will be packed? No, it doesn't. Times change and every season at Walt Disney World can bring about different touring patterns, so make your daily plans according to what works best for you. Please use the following chart as a general guide:

Park	Busiest Days of the week
Magic Kingdom	Monday, Thursday, Saturday
Animal Kingdom	Friday
Disney's Hollywood Studios	Tuesday
Epcot	Sunday, Wednesday

Crowd size is another factor that will affect your trip. Walt Disney World has different "seasons" of the year. These seasons are based upon attendance levels in the parks. Obviously, the "peak seasons", or highest attendance times of the year, are when school is out or on vacation. Thus, Easter/Spring Break, summer, and Christmas are the busiest times to vacation. If you have the opportunity, it is generally cheaper and less crowded during non-peak season times. Listed below is a chart of seasonal attendance. This chart is just an estimate, not exact, as crowd levels can vary yearly.

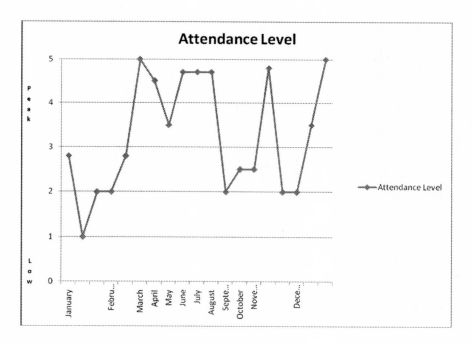

Special Events

Each season has special activities that occur throughout the year. There are many smaller events that happen every day so I will try to focus on the major events that are planned each month (specific dates will vary year to year). This may also help guide you in deciding when you want to visit Walt Disney World:

• *Year of a Million Dreams*—a promotion where "dreams" (anything from special Mickey Ears, Dream FASTPASSES, or an overnight stay in Cinderella Castle) may be bestowed upon guests by Cast Members.

- **January**
  - Walt Disney World Marathon
- **End of February**
  - Atlanta Braves Spring Training at Disney's Wide World of Sports
- **March**
  - Atlanta Braves Spring Training
  - ESPN the Weekend
  - Easter Holiday Events
- **April**
  - Epcot's Flower & Garden Festival
- **May**
  - Epcot's Flower & Garden Festival
- **June**
  - Epcot's Flower & Garden Festival
  - Star Wars Weekends
- **July**
  - Fourth of July Holiday Events
- **August**
  - Pirate & Princess Party
- **September**
  - Night of Joy
  - Epcot's Food & Wine Festival
  - Mickey's Not So Scary Halloween Party
- **October**
  - Epcot's Food & Wine Festival

- Mickey's Not So Scary Halloween Party

- **November**

  - Golf Classic at Walt Disney World
  - Epcot's Food & Wine Festival
  - Festival of the Masters
  - ABC's Super Soap Weekend
  - Thanksgiving Holiday Events
  - Christmas Holiday Events

    - Osborne Family Spectacle of Lights
    - Mickey's Very Merry Christmas Party
    - Holidays around the World
    - Candlelight Processional

- **December**

  - Christmas Holiday Events

    - Osborne Family Spectacle of Lights
    - Mickey's Very Merry Christmas Party
    - Holidays around the World
    - Candlelight Processional

  - Pleasure Island's New Year's Eve
  - Atlantic Dance Hall's New Years Eve

Traveling to Walt Disney World is another key issue when you are planning. I will not attempt to tell you how you should travel to Walt Disney World. Everyone has their own needs and considerations, so I will attempt to give you some general things to consider. The main issue is how are you going to get there. That is determined by several factors:

- ***Will you be flying or driving to Walt Disney World?***

- There are so many airlines and web sites around that if you are flexible with your dates, and have an idea in advance of when you might be vacationing, you can usually find a decent deal.

- Does your home airport charge you to park your car?

- How expensive is the cost of gas per gallon?

- Do you need a car when you are at Walt Disney World?

- If so, how much does it cost to rent a car during your time of the year?

- By driving it usually allows you to take more items of need. If this is important then driving may be a better option.

- *What time of the year are you traveling?*

  - If you travel during the lower attendance seasons you may find cheaper airfare and cheaper resort rates

If you choose to fly to Orlando there are a few things you need to know. Orlando International Airport (MCO) has more than 35 million visitors each year and 96,000 pass through it daily. Because of this, it is a destination for several major airlines. The major airlines are:

Airline	Website	Phone
Aero Mexico	www.aeromexico.com	1-800-237-6639
Air Canada	www.aircanada.com	1-800-247-2262
Air Tran	www.airtran.com	1-800-247-8726
Alaska	www.alaskaair.com	1-800-252-7522
American	www.aa.com	1-800-433-7300
ATA	www.ata.com	1-800-225-2995
British Airways	www.britishairways.com	1-800-247-9297
Continental	www.continental.com	1-800-525-0280
Delta	www.delta.com	1-800-221-1212
Frontier	www.frontierairlines.com	1-800-432-1359
Jet Blue	www.jetblue.com	1-800-538-2583
Lufthansa	www.lufthansa.com	1-800-645-3880

Northwest	www.nwa.com	1-800-225-2525
Southwest	www.southwest.com	1-800-435-9792
Ted	www.flyted.com	1-800-225-5833
United	www.united.com	1-800-241-6522
US Airways	www.usairways.com	1-800-428-4322

Once you arrive at Orlando International Airport (MCO) you have a few options to get from the airport to Walt Disney World.

Disney's Magical Express

The first method may be the easiest, Disney's Magical Express. Any guest who is staying at a Walt Disney World resort gets free complimentary use of this service. Magical Express is a busing service that will transfer guests from Orlando International Airport to their Walt Disney World Resort and back to the airport at the end of your stay. A few weeks before you leave your hometown's airport you will need to call Disney and inform them that you are going to take advantage of Disney's Magical Express. Disney will send you unique tags to put on your bags. When you arrive in Orlando, your bags will be taken by Disney to your resort for you. You will never have to touch them. (You could choose to just use the bus service and take your luggage with you as another option). Disney's Magical Express bus will then take you back to the airport on your departure day. The Magical Express ride can take anywhere from forty-five minutes to two hours depending on the number of resort stops. Seldom will a bus have guests staying at more than three or four resorts. Once again, Disney has made everything stress-free for their guests. Disney's Magical Express is located on the B-side of the Main Terminal on Ground Transportation (Level One).

If you choose to not utilize Disney's Magical Express you have three other options: Rental Car, taxi, or shuttle.

Rental Car

A rental car's price range is determined by several factors such as car type, day of the week, and time of year. Orlando International Airport has several rental car agencies available on site and they are located in Terminals A and B:

Car Company	Website	Phone
Alamo	www.alamo.com	1-800-327-9633
Avis	www.avis.com	1-800-831-2847
Budget	www.budget.com	1-800-527-0700
Dollar	www.dollar.com	1-800-800-4000
L and M	www.lmcarrental.com	1-800-277-5171
National	www.nationalcar.com	1-800-227-7368

Taxi

A taxi will run about $40-$60 for a family (it may carry up to nine passengers), and carry the same rate regardless of the number of passengers. The following Taxi companies operate at Orlando International Airport (MCO):

Taxi Company	Phone
Ace Metro/Luxury Cab	(407) 855-1111
Diamond Cab Company	(407) 523-3333
Star Taxi	(407) 857-9999
Town & Country Transport	(407) 828-3035
Yellow/City Cab	(407) 422-2222

Shuttle

Mears Transportation Group is the company that runs the shuttle service from MCO. Shuttle van fares are charged per person. It is advisable to check with the attendant for round-trip fares and children's rates. Shuttle vans are available at several locations: both the A and B sides of the Main Terminal, on the Ground Transportation Level (Level One), and at various commercial parking spaces.

The following are approximate rates for taxi and shuttle service. Please call to check for exact rates.

Destination	Taxi (per trip) (one way)	Shuttle Van (per person) (One way/Round Trip)
Airport Hotels	$12	$11/$16

International Drive	$33-$39	$17/$27
Downtown Orlando	$35	$16/$26
Lake Buena Vista	$47	$19/$31
Kissimmee	$43-$60	$25/$43
Walt Disney World	$60	$19/$31
Port Canaveral	$105	
Chauffeured Limousine	$50–$85 per hour	

Now that you have made it to Disney you need to understand the transportation system that Disney provides guests. There are three major means of transportation: Bus, Boats, and Monorail.

Buses

Disney has buses that will transport you from the parks to your resort and back. This is the main mode of transportation to get guests around the World. Check with your resort for up-to-date information. Buses traditionally run every twenty minutes or so thus providing guests with normally no longer than a half hour wait time at the most. Obviously if you are traveling during the peak seasons, the bus wait times may vary slightly. Buses will start their routes about an hour before each park opens and up to two hours after closing time. Again this varies from season to season. Buses also travel to Downtown Disney (DTD) and the Ticket and Transportation Center (TTC) near the Magic Kingdom. If there is no direct link between where you are and your destination, you can take a bus to either location, and then make a connecting bus route. For example, Disney does not run buses from one resort to another, so you would need to connect at Ticket and Transportation Center or Downtown Disney. Another option is to take a bus from your resort location to a nearby park, then take a bus from that park to another resort.

Boats

Several Walt Disney World resorts offer water transportation to and from resorts and the parks. This mode of transportation is not the fastest, as you will make several stops along the way, but it is a relaxing way to cool down and enjoy the scenery that is offered. Here are the resorts/locations which offer boat service to the parks:

- *Magic Kingdom*—from Wilderness Lodge, Fort Wilderness, and Ticket and Transportation Center

- *Disney's Hollywood Studios*—from Yacht & Beach Club, Boardwalk, Swan and Dolphin and Epcot

- *Epcot*—from Yacht & Beach Club, Boardwalk, Swan and Dolphin and Disney's Hollywood Studios

- *Downtown Disney*—from Saratoga Springs, Port Orleans Riverside and Port Orleans French Quarter

Monorail

The last means of transportation is maybe the most famous, the monorail. The monorail runs from these three resorts:

- *Grand Floridian*—to Magic Kingdom, Contemporary, Ticket and Transportation Center and Polynesian Resort

- *Polynesian*—to Grand Floridian, Magic Kingdom, Contemporary, and Ticket and Transportation Center

- *Contemporary*—to Magic Kingdom, Grand Floridian, Polynesian, and Ticket and Transportation Center

Once at the Ticket and Transportation Center, you can switch to another monorail that will take you to Epcot

Guest Services

Walt Disney World offers about every type of service a guest would need. Here are some of the major guest services that are provided:

- **ATM**—Located at every resort and theme park

- **Baby Care Facilities**—Located at every theme park

- **Babysitting Service**—This is called "Kids Night Out." Disney provides a babysitter to come and stay with your children in your resort room. You can make reservations by calling 407-828-0920. Rates for this service run about

$15 per hour and additional children run a few dollars more. Please call Disney for exact rates.

- **Childcare Facilities**—Many Deluxe resorts offer this type of care for children ages 4-12 who are toilet trained. You can make reservations by calling 407-WDW-DINE. The rate is about $11 per hour per child. The Polynesian is home to Peter Pan's Neverland Club, Beach Club has the Sandcastle Club, Wilderness Lodge offers the Cub's Den, and Animal Kingdom Lodge has Simba's Clubhouse. Call the resort directly to ask them if they are open and taking reservations. These facilities offer board games, video games, movies, arts and crafts, dinner, and more.

- **First Aid**—Each park has a first aid station. If you have an emergency or a medical condition, find any Disney Cast Member and ask for assistance. If you have special needs at your resort or for your room, contact the resort directly.

- **Guests with Disabilities**—Disney offers motorized scooters and wheelchairs for those who may have difficulty traveling throughout Walt Disney World. The Disney buses are also capable of transporting scooters and wheelchairs. Each park offers rentals of these for the day. You can call Disney at 407-939-7807 for more details.

- **Kennels**—Disney is home to the Kennel Club where guests can board their pet as needed. Reservations are required and prices vary. Please call Disney for specific details and rules for boarding.

- **Lockers**—Lockers are located at the entrance of each park. There is a minimal charge associated with using these lockers. A locker rental can make all the difference in your day if you store extra clothes or other items you have purchased throughout the day.

- **Shipping Packages**—There are two methods of shipping packages, one to the front of the park you are visiting and one back to your resort.

  - If you purchase something, but do not want to carry it around the park all day, you can request to have it sent to the front of the park to guest relations. As you leave the park for the day you can stop by, pick it up, and take it with you.

  - The other method is to have Disney ship the package back to your room. This system is convenient as long as you give it a day or so to get there. When you make your purchase just let them know you would like to have it delivered to your room. You will give the Cast Member your information. It's that simple.

- **Stroller Rental**—There are areas in each park where you can rent strollers for your children for the day. Check the park maps for exact locations, but most are just at the entrance of each park. Stroller rental seems to increase in cost each trip so check for exact rates. The cost is around $10, and if you return the stroller to the location you will receive $1 back. Double strollers run about $15 and allow for more storage for your items if necessary. You will receive a card with your name on it to put into a compartment on the stroller. That way when you park your stroller outside an attraction others will know whose stroller is whose.

  - One added perk is that if you rent a stroller at one park and then travel to another park that same day, you can show your receipt and get a stroller rental free at the next park since you had already paid for the day.

Ticket Options

Choosing your tickets is an important decision. You would think that you could just say, "I will be at Walt Disney World for five nights, so I need a five day ticket." Unfortunately it isn't that easy. In 2005 Disney made a change to their ticketing system that allows for more individualization. You now have greater choice and can customize your ticket to fit your needs. The system is called *Magic Your Way*. The tickets start off as a base ticket allowing you to enter a park each day. That is the simple part. The next sections that follow may seem a bit complex, but I will attempt to give them some simplicity.

The first thing you will need to do is choose how many days you will need. Once you have selected that you are ready to begin. *Magic Your Way* tickets are available for purchase for one day up to ten days. If your stay extends beyond ten days you would have to purchase another *Magic Your Way* ticket for the remaining days of your trip. With a base ticket, whatever park you choose to enter is the only park you can attend that day. The next day you are able to go to another park if you want or even back to previous park. (Prices are subject to change)

Magic Your Way Base Tickets

Number of Days	Price
1 Day Adult Ticket—Age 10 +	$75.62

1 Day Child Ticket—Age 3-9	$63.90
2 Day Adult Ticket—Age 10 +	$148.04
2 Day Child Ticket—Age 3-9	$124.61
3 Day Adult Ticket—Age 10 +	$216.20
3 Day Child Ticket—Age 3-9	$182.12
4 Day Adult Ticket—Age 10 +	$225.78
4 Day Child Ticket—Age 3-9	$189.57
5 Day Adult Ticket—Age 10 +	$228.98
5 Day Child Ticket—Age 3-9	$190.64
6 Day Adult Ticket—Age 10 +	$231.11
6 Day Child Ticket—Age 3-9	$192.77
7 Day Adult Ticket—Age 10 +	$223.24
7 Day Child Ticket—Age 3-9	$193.83
8 Day Adult Ticket—Age 10 +	$235.37
8 Day Child Ticket—Age 3-9	$197.03
9 Day Adult Ticket—Age 10 +	$237.50
9 Day Child Ticket—Age 3-9	$198.09
10 Day Adult Ticket—Age 10 +	$239.63
10 Day Child Ticket—Age 3-9	$199.16

There are several options that you can choose to add to your Magic Your Way ticket if you need them. Each will add to the cost of your ticket.

Option #1—Park Hopper

• **Park Hopper option allows you to enter more than one park per day**

Magic Your Way Park Hopper Tickets

Number of Days	Price
1 Day Adult Ticket—Age 10 +	$123.54

1 Day Child Ticket—Age 3-9	$111.83
2 Day Adult Ticket—Age 10 +	$195.96
2 Day Child Ticket—Age 3-9	$172.53
3 Day Adult Ticket—Age 10 +	$264.12
3 Day Child Ticket—Age 3-9	$230.04
4 Day Adult Ticket—Age 10 +	$273.71
4 Day Child Ticket—Age 3-9	$237.50
5 Day Adult Ticket—Age 10 +	$276.90
5 Day Child Ticket—Age 3-9	$238.56
6 Day Adult Ticket—Age 10 +	$279.03
6 Day Child Ticket—Age 3-9	$240.69
7 Day Adult Ticket—Age 10 +	$281.16
7 Day Child Ticket—Age 3-9	$241.76
8 Day Adult Ticket—Age 10 +	$283.29
8 Day Child Ticket—Age 3-9	$244.95
9 Day Adult Ticket—Age 10 +	$285.42
9 Day Child Ticket—Age 3-9	$246.02
10 Day Adult Ticket—Age 10 +	$287.55
10 Day Child Ticket—Age 3-9	$247.08

Option #2—Water Park & Fun Option

- **Allows you access to Disney's Blizzard Beach& Typhoon Lagoon Water Parks, Disney's Wide World of Sports Complex, Disney Quest, and Pleasure Island**

Magic Your Way Water Park & Fun Tickets

Number of Days	Price
1 Day Adult Ticket—Age 10 +	$128.88
1 Day Child Ticket—Age 3-9	$117.16

2 Day Adult Ticket—Age 10 +	$201.29
2 Day Child Ticket—Age 3-9	$177.87
3 Day Adult Ticket—Age 10 +	$269.46
3 Day Child Ticket—Age 3-9	$235.38
4 Day Adult Ticket—Age 10 +	$279.05
4 Day Child Ticket—Age 3-9	$242.83
5 Day Adult Ticket—Age 10 +	$282.24
5 Day Child Ticket—Age 3-9	$243.90
6 Day Adult Ticket—Age 10 +	$284.37
6 Day Child Ticket—Age 3-9	$246.04
7 Day Adult Ticket—Age 10 +	$286.50
7 Day Child Ticket—Age 3-9	$247.10
8 Day Adult Ticket—Age 10 +	$288.63
8 Day Child Ticket—Age 3-9	$250.29
9 Day Adult Ticket—Age 10 +	$290.76
9 Day Child Ticket—Age 3-9	$251.36
10 Day Adult Ticket—Age 10 +	$292.89
10 Day Child Ticket—Age 3-9	$252.42

Option #3—Park Hopper & Water Park & Fun Option

- **Allows you to park hop, as well as allowing access to Disney's Blizzard Beach &Typhoon Lagoon Water Parks, Disney's Wide World of Sports Complex, Disney Quest, and Pleasure Island**

Magic Your Way Park Hopper & Water Park & Fun Tickets

Number of Days	Price
1 Day Adult Ticket—Age 10 +	$176.80
1 Day Child Ticket—Age 3-9	$165.09
2 Day Adult Ticket—Age 10 +	$249.23

2 Day Child Ticket—Age 3-9	$225.79
3 Day Adult Ticket—Age 10 +	$317.39
3 Day Child Ticket—Age 3-9	$283.31
4 Day Adult Ticket—Age 10 +	$326.97
4 Day Child Ticket—Age 3-9	$290.76
5 Day Adult Ticket—Age 10 +	$330.16
5 Day Child Ticket—Age 3-9	$291.83
6 Day Adult Ticket—Age 10 +	$332.30
6 Day Child Ticket—Age 3-9	$293.96
7 Day Adult Ticket—Age 10 +	$334.43
7 Day Child Ticket—Age 3-9	$295.02
8 Day Adult Ticket—Age 10 +	$336.56
8 Day Child Ticket—Age 3-9	$298.21
9 Day Adult Ticket—Age 10 +	$338.69
9 Day Child Ticket—Age 3-9	$299.28
10 Day Adult Ticket—Age 10 +	$340.82
10 Day Child Ticket—Age 3-9	$300.34

Option #4—No Expiration

- **By purchasing this add on you may use any unused days on this ticket for future vacations.**

Magic Your Way No Expiration Tickets

Number of Days	Price
2 Day Adult Ticket—Age 10 +	$164.01
2 Day Child Ticket—Age 3-9	$140.58
3 Day Adult Ticket—Age 10 +	$237.50
3 Day Child Ticket—Age 3-9	$203.42

4 Day Adult Ticket—Age 10 +	$273.71
4 Day Child Ticket—Age 3-9	$237.50
5 Day Adult Ticket—Age 10 +	$292.88
5 Day Child Ticket—Age 3-9	$254.54
6 Day Adult Ticket—Age 10 +	$300.33
6 Day Child Ticket—Age 3-9	$261.99
7 Day Adult Ticket—Age 10 +	$334.41
7 Day Child Ticket—Age 3-9	$295.01
8 Day Adult Ticket—Age 10 +	$373.82
8 Day Child Ticket—Age 3-9	$335.48
9 Day Adult Ticket—Age 10 +	$402.57
9 Day Child Ticket—Age 3-9	$363.17
10 Day Adult Ticket—Age 10 +	$431.33
10 Day Child Ticket—Age 3-9	$390.86

Option #5—Annual Pass

• This provides you with 365 days of admittance to Walt Disney World parks. I am sure you are saying, "I can't go to Disney that many days." That is ok. If you are planning on a trip that lasts longer than ten days, or maybe two trips to Disney in a year, the Annual Pass may be for you. An added perk is that throughout the year Disney will offer Annual Passholders special room discounts. These are not guaranteed, but in our experience Disney has offered them most times of the year.

Annual Pass Tickets

Annual Pass	Price
Adult Ticket—Age 10 +	$477.12
Child Ticket—Age 3-9	$420.68

Option #6—Premium Annual Pass

- **Same as Annual Pass with added features such as access to Disney's Blizzard Beach& Typhoon Lagoon Water Parks, Disney's Wide World of Sports Complex, Disney Quest, and Pleasure Island**

Premium Annual Pass Tickets

Premium Annual Pass	Price
Adult Ticket—Age 10 +	$616.66
Child Ticket—Age 3-9	$543.17

Vacation Package

Disney also offers vacation packages. You have a choice of how to book your vacation. Vacation packages are different from "room only" reservations. "Room only" reservations are just what the title states, you are paying for the room portion, not the tickets. With a package you are getting park tickets, as well as your resort, for one price. We have found that many times it is cheaper to book a "room only" reservation and get park tickets separately. It is always a good idea to price things separately then compare that with a package. The other option a Disney package offers is an add-on such as the Disney Dining Plan. We will discuss this option in more detail in Chapter Five. Disney continually adjusts their packages so it is advisable to check the official Disney website often.

Now it is time to book your vacation. How do you do it? The choices seem endless, but here are a few of the major options you have:

- *Book the trip yourself through the Disney website* (www.disneyworld.com) or *by phone* 407-939-7675

    - Both ways will offer you the same deals, although we have found that sometimes if one method says there is no availability, give the other option a try.

- *Use an authorized Disney Travel Agent*

    - Disney allows certain travel agencies the ability to be deemed, "Disney-authorized vacation planners".

    - These people are not employees of Disney, but rather are recognized as respected agents.

- The benefit of using a travel agent is that they can plan everything for you. You don't have to worry about every little detail.

- *Use a service such as AAA or AARP*

  - If you are a member of an organization such as AAA or AARP make sure that you ask about any possible discounts or vacation packages.

The next thing you need to do before you go is to have a general idea of the cost. We won't get into specific budget plans as everyone has different monetary issues. Family size, age of children, and time of year may all be factors in your price. There are too many variables to be able to give an exact cost.

WDW Peak Season Advice

- Find the time of the year you want to travel

- Figure out how many will be traveling

- Compare airfare for that time of the year from different airfare carriers vs. gas for driving, meals and possible hotel stay for a night

- Choose the number of days you will stay at Walt Disney World (resort/hotel)

- Figure the cost of tickets for each person

- Add in the cost of meals and snacks each day—a general guideline is to figure $50 per adult and about $25-$30 per child.

After you have all these totals added together you can then decide on various options to make your stay cheaper or more expensive depending on how much money you have allowed for your vacation.

Here are some variables that you can compare or change to possibly save money or extend your vacation:

- *Length of stay*

  - If you choose to stay at a cheaper priced resort (Value instead of a Deluxe) not only will save money, but you could in fact extend your vacation by a few days by using the savings for an added night or two

- *What type of tickets do you need?*

- There are all sorts of options that we will discuss later, but you can find savings here depending on the type of options you want for your family

- *How much will we spend on meals?*

  - This may be the biggest factor. There are so many options to choose from at Walt Disney World. The general guide is $50 per adult per day and $25-$30 per child per day. This figure though can vary greatly depending on the type of meal (s) you pick.

  - Meal plans such as Disney's Dining Plan may save your family money depending on the restaurants you choose. Don't forget to factor in snack and drinks as well.

3

Choosing your resort

Choosing the perfect resort for your trip might seem impossible with all of the choices in the area. Should you stay on Disney property or off-site? How much should you spend on accommodations? How much time will you be in the room? Do you simply want a resting place or a home away from home? Is service important to you? The questions could go on and on. This overview should help guide you in your decision making.

Off-Site

There are hundreds of off-site hotels in the Orlando area. We want to focus on four main areas of hotels near Walt Disney World.

Hotel Plaza Boulevard

The first location is the Hotel Plaza Boulevard near Downtown Disney. These seven hotels put you right in the heart of Downtown Disney. These hotels are technically on Walt Disney World property, but you should not expect the perks that you receive by staying at a Walt Disney World resort. Most of these hotels are similar to the moderate and even some Deluxe Disney resorts. Many times these resorts will offer deals or specials that can make it advantageous to stay there instead of at a Disney resort. These hotels offer a few amenities that are different from the other Orlando area hotels:

- Complimentary shuttle service to Walt Disney World theme parks, water parks and other attractions—**but note that the shuttles do not operate as frequently as Disney transportation.**

- Disney tickets available for purchase at each hotel

- Advance tee times and discounts at all five Disney golf courses

- Disney gift stores located in each of the resorts in Orlando

- Priority seating for Walt Disney World Resort dinner shows and theme park restaurants

- Passport to Savings with exclusive discounts and specials on dining, entertainment and shopping

- Walking distance of Downtown Disney

Resort	Website	Phone	Price Range
Best Western Lake Buena Vista Resort	www.bestwestern.com	(407) 828-2424	$110–$225
Buena Vista Palace Hotel & Spa	www.buenavistapalace.com	1-866-397-6516	$99–$189
Doubletree Guest Suites	www.Doubletree.hilton.com	(407) 934-1000	$120–$200
Hilton Orlando	www.hilton.com	(407) 827-3890	$115–$225
Holiday Inn	www.ichotelsgroup.com	1-888-HOLIDAY	$99–$179
Regal Sun (Formerly Grosvenor Resort)	www.regalsunresort.com	1-800-624-4109	$89–$199
Royal Plaza	www.royalplaza.com	(407) 828-2828	$120–$199

International Drive

This is one of the more populated areas for those venturing to other Orlando area attractions. There are a few nice hotels in this area such as:

Resort	Website	Phone	Price Range
Embassy Suites	www.hilton.com	407-352-1400	$125–$250
Peabody	www.peabodyorlando.com	407-352-4000	$150–$400

Because of the heavy traffic in this area, discounts and cheaper resort rates are abundant. Travel time to and from the parks will be much longer than normal.

Kissimmee Area

This area is closest in travel time to Walt Disney World outside of the Downtown Disney resorts. These hotels will cost a bit more than the International Drive hotels, but the added cost may be worth it. There is less traffic in this area as well as a nicer quality of hotel. A few top choices are:

Resort	Website	Phone	Price Range
Celebration Hotel	www.celebrationhotel.com	407-566-1844	$115–$250
Quality Suites Maingate	www.choicehotels.com	407-396-8040	$79–$179
Serlago Hotel (formerly Holiday Inn and Suites Maingate East)	www.orlando-family-fun-hotel.com	407-396-3488	$89–$179

Lake Buena Vista Area

The Lake Buena Vista area is very close to Downtown Disney. This area seems to have more suites and villa-type rooms available than any other off-site location. Some of the top hotels are:

Resort	Website	Phone	Price Range
Buena Vista Suites	www.buenavistasuites.com	1-800-537-7737	$99–$299
Holiday Inn Sun-spree Resort	www.holiday-inn.com	407-239-4500	$125–$199
Sheraton Safari Hotel	www.starwood.com	407-239-0444	$110–$250
Sheraton Vistana Resort	www.starwood.com	407-239-3100	$115–$225

One other option is to rent a vacation home or condominium for your trip. These are popping up all over the Orlando area and offer a much larger room capacity for vacationers and many times at a much cheaper price than those on-site. You may be able to rent a three bed-room home for a week for the cost of 2-3 nights staying on property. This is very helpful in saving money if you then divide the cost of rental among two families that could fit in that house. The drawback though is the travel time to and from the parks, paying for parking, no perks such as EMH, and finally no Disney atmosphere around you all the time.

Some of these hotels are great, but many are in less than ideal locations. If you stay off-site, whether at a seedy hotel or a fancy condo, keep in mind you do not have the Disney theme around you. If you are going to Walt Disney World and Disney is your main destination, you may want to be immersed in Disney. Staying off-site cannot give you that magical Disney feeling. Many will also tell you that they are, "just minutes from Disney" and that they offer a "free shuttle" to the parks. Let's sort through this type of advertising. To start, the Walt Disney World property is vast and roughly 47 sq. miles. When these hotels claim that they are "minutes from Disney" that may be "as the crow flies". You have to factor in traffic, stoplights, and any other delays. You are not mere "minutes away". Also these claims are only to the entrance to Walt Disney World. Once you reach that, you still have to travel 10-15 minutes to reach the actual park.

Now let's talk about the "free shuttle". Most of these hotels run a shuttle to and from the Walt Disney World parks. The problem is they don't seat many people at a time, they don't run very frequently, and they are not allowed to drop guests off as close to the park entrances as Disney transportation. If you have a car and drive to the parks that will help some, but you still have to pay for parking each day.

Please note that we are not experts on the off-site hotels. If you would like further details about other Orlando area hotels there are plenty of web sites and books that can provide you with much more specific hotel information. We are just spoiled by the quality and service of Disney accommodations.

On-Site

Now we're talking. Let me say something right away, we are not affiliated with Disney. We get nothing by speaking well of Disney. All we are doing is providing you with advice and experiences as to what will give someone the best Walt Disney World vacation. If you will be traveling to Walt Disney World during the peak seasons, on-site resort rooms will fill up fairly quickly. It is imperative that you call as soon as you know you will be vacationing at Walt Disney World.

We feel that staying on-site gives vacationers at Disney the best experience possible. Staying on-site allows guests to use Disney transportation. They run buses from Disney resorts to the front of each park. The buses usually will arrive every 15-20 minutes. There are many people who love their cars, but when you travel during peak times, it is nice to not have to hassle with driving around through traffic after a busy day at the parks. Disney also offers other modes of transportation such as ferries, boats, and monorails. These are fun to ride at any time. The key to Disney transportation is that they run from 1-2 hours prior to the parks opening and 1-2 hours after the parks close. After a long day it is nice to just walk (stagger) back to the bus stop and have someone else pick you up and drop you off right at the front of your resort.

The most important difference in staying on-site is how convenient it is to go back to your resort during the day and then return to the parks in the evening. If you get to the parks early, you may want to go back to your resort in the afternoon to swim, relax, or take a nap. Later in the day when you are recharged and want to go back to the parks after your rest period, you just walk out front of your resort again and catch the bus for the park. It is very simple and easy. If you are staying off-site, you are less apt to go back to your hotel/condo because of the hassle of driving to and from the park again that day.

In 2008 Walt Disney World updated their resort pricing information. Disney has five seasons at which it offers different rates: value, regular, summer, peak, and holiday. Disney now prices rooms each night, just as most hotels presently do. This varies from the past, when Disney would charge your entire stay based on the price of the season in which you checked in. Disney has changed that policy so that even if you overlap seasons you may pay a different price each night of your stay. The days of every night of your trip being the same price are gone. Disney has also upped the price for weekend stays (Friday and Saturday). These days will now cost more per night than weekday stays.

EMH

Extra Magic Hours (EMH) is another perk available for Walt Disney World Resort guests. Each day there is one resort that will have EMH in the morning, where the park opens up one hour early for guests staying on-site. In a peak season this is the key to your survival in the parks. EMH is also offered at one park each day in the evening. The park stays open three hours later for Walt Disney World resort guests. You must show your room key and obtain a wristband in order to stay in the park. EMH's allow certain rides to be available to those guests. The EMH benefit might be the main key to staying on-property vs. staying off-site. If you are traveling during any of the peak seasons utilizing this method of touring is a must. The Magic Kingdom has even been known to stay open until 5:00 AM!

WDW Peak Season Advice

Do:

- Stay On-Property

- Take advantage of the perks of staying On-Property

- Utilize Extra Magic Hours

- Take a break in the afternoon to go back to your resort

- Return in the evening when others who stayed the whole day are exhausted and leaving.

- Use Disney Transportation to visit other resorts

- Use Disney Transportation as a fun way to break up your day. Ride in the monorail, ferry or boat to get a different view of Walt Disney World

Don't:

- Stay off-site, at least not your first few visits

- Fall for the "Free Shuttle" and "Minutes from Disney" advertising you will see from off-site hotels

There are four different classes of resorts at Walt Disney World: *Value* (Cheapest Room Cost), *Moderate* (Mid-Level Room Cost), *Deluxe* (Most Expensive Room Cost), and *Disney Vacation Club Resorts* (which are similar in cost to the Deluxe). The first thing you will need to do is to decide which type of room you can afford. ***Please note that beginning in 2008, Disney changed its policy and will start to calculate rates on a day-by-day basis.***

Value Resorts

The Values are the cheapest, have the smallest room types, and offer the least amenities. There are four value resorts: *All-Star Sports*, *All-Star Music*, *All-Star Movies*, and *Pop Century*. Main details about each value resort are as follows:

- ***All-Star Movies***

    - Phone-407-939-7000

- Price Range-$82-$150
- Closest Park-Animal Kingdom
- Number of rooms-1,920
- Room Size-Approximately 260 square feet
- Most rooms have two double beds
- Theme of Resort-Disney Movies with building featuring 101Dalmations, Toy Story, Fantasia, The Mighty Ducks, and Herbie.
- Food/Dining-Food Court
- Pools-Two themed pools: Mighty Ducks pool which has a hockey theme & the Fantasia pool with a Mickey statue

- *All-Star Music*
  - Phone-407-939-6000
  - Price Range-$82-$150
  - Closest Park-Animal Kingdom
  - Number of rooms-1,920
  - Room Size-Approximately 260 square feet
  - Most rooms have two double beds
  - Limited number of Family Suites
  - Theme of Resort-Music with buildings featuring musical instruments
  - Food/Dining-Food Court
  - Pools-Two themed pools: Piano pool with an Ariel statue & the Calypso pool shaped like a guitar featuring Donald and friends

- *All-Star Sports*
  - Phone-407-939-5000
  - Price Range-$82-$150
  - Closest Park-Animal Kingdom
  - Number of rooms-1,920
  - Room Size-Approximately 260 square feet

- Most rooms have two double beds
- Theme of Resort-Sports with buildings featuring basketball, football, tennis, surfboards, and baseball icons
- Food/Dining-Food Court
- Pools-Two themed pools: Surfboard pool & Grand Slam Baseball pool

- *Pop Century*
  - Phone-407-938-4000
  - Price Range-$82-$150
  - Closest Park-Epcot
  - Number of rooms-2,880
  - Room Size-Approximately 260 square feet
  - Most rooms have two double beds
  - Theme of Resort-Popular Culture from 1960-Present. The 50's buildings feature a jukebox, bowling pins, and Lady and the Tramp. The 60's buildings feature Play-Doh, yo-yo's, and Jungle Book characters. The 70's buildings feature a Big-Wheel, Mickey Mouse, and an 8-Track tape player as icons. The 80's buildings have a Rubik's Cube and Walkman icons. The 90's buildings feature a Cell Phone and laptop computer as icons.
  - Food/Dining-Food Court & Bar
  - Pools-Three themed pools: 70's Hippy Dippy pool with flower shaped silhouettes, the 50's Bowling Pin pool themed around a bowling alley, and the 80's-90's Computer themed pool

Each has a unique theme throughout the resort and are perfect for all ages. The colorful décor and larger-than-life Disney icons are special touches to the Value resorts. Pop Century is the largest, but also the newest of the values resorts. The food courts and arcades will please children. Well-themed swimming pools are also eye-catching. The question you have to ask yourself first is how much time will you be spending in your room? The value resorts are a great choice for anyone who will be spending most of their time in the parks and would like the benefits of staying on-site while paying the least for their accommodations. You can stay a few days longer at Walt Disney World by the savings you may get by staying at a value resort.

Moderate Resorts

The Moderates are the next price level for Disney resorts. The moderate resorts are *Caribbean Beach*, *Coronado Springs*, and *Port Orleans Riverside* and *French Quarter*. Main details about each resort are as follows:

- *Caribbean Beach*
    - Phone-407-934-3400
    - Price Range-$149-$240
    - Closest Park-Epcot
    - Number of rooms-2,112
    - Room Size-Approximately 340 square feet
    - Most rooms have two double beds
    - Theme of Resort-Village in the Caribbean
    - Food/Dining-Food Court, small grocery store, & sit-down restaurant
    - Pool-One large themed pool & each building has its own quiet pool: The large themed pool is shared by the entire resort. It resembles a Spanish Fort. It features waterslides, a waterfall, and water cannons. The smaller pools service each building/area of the resort

- *Coronado Springs*
    - Phone-407-939-1000
    - Price Range-$149-$240
    - Closest Park-Animal Kingdom
    - Number of rooms-1,967
    - Room Size-Approximately 314 square feet
    - Most rooms have two double beds
    - Theme of Resort-Southwest/Mexico
    - Food/Dining-Food Court, counter service restaurant, lounge, & sit-down restaurant
    - Pool-One large themed pool & three smaller pools: The main pool is the Mayan Pyramid pool. The theme is an ancient Mayan Temple. It features a

water slide, children's pool and sand box. The three smaller pools service each building/area of the resort.

- ***Port Orleans French Quarter***
  - Phone-407-934-5000
  - Price Range-$149-$240
  - Closest Park-Epcot & Downtown Disney Area
  - Number of rooms-1,000
  - Room Size-Approximately 314 square feet
  - Most rooms have two double beds
  - Theme of Resort-New Orleans/Mardi Gras
  - Food/Dining-Food Court
  - Pool-One large themed pool: This pool features a serpent water slide, and alligator water fountains.

- ***Port Orleans Riverside***
  - Phone-407-934-6000
  - Price Range-$149-$240
  - Closest Park-Epcot & Downtown Disney Area
  - Number of rooms-2,048
  - Room Size-Approximately 314 square feet
  - Most rooms have two double beds
  - Theme of Resort-Southern US/Mississippi. Buildings are set to resemble southern mansions
  - Food/Dining-Food Court & sit-down restaurant
  - Pool-One large themed pool & five smaller pools: The main pool is features a water slide, kiddie pool, and a geyser. The five smaller pools service each building/area of the resort.

These resort rooms are bigger than the values and offer a few more amenities. These resorts each have a unique theme to them, but not quite as over-the-top as the Value Resorts. Again, themed pools can be found on each property. Rooms will cost anywhere from \$149–\$240 depending on your vacation season. One extra note is that Coronado Springs has a convention center and thus can have more crowds at its resort at certain times of the year than the other moderates.

Swan and Dolphin

Before we get to the Deluxe Resorts, there are two other resorts that are located on the Disney property and get some of the Disney perks such as EMH and Disney transportation. These resorts are the Swan and Dolphin.

Resort	Website	Phone	Price Range
Walt Disney World Swan	www.swandolphin.com	407-934-3000	\$125–\$299
Walt Disney World Dolphin	www.swandolphin.com	407-934-4000	\$125–\$299

The downside to these resorts is that they are not owned by Disney. While you do get a few perks staying here, the cost is in the range of the deluxe resorts, and you cannot use Disney's Magical Express from Orlando International Airport, or charge items on your room key. These two resorts are located in the Epcot area and range in costs from \$259-\$400.

Deluxe Resorts

The Deluxe resorts are: *Animal Kingdom Lodge, Beach Club & Yacht Club, Boardwalk Inn, Contemporary, Grand Floridian, Polynesian,* and *Wilderness Lodge.* These are the most expensive, but have the largest rooms and the most amenities. These resorts can range in price depending on the type of room you choose and the season you vacation in. Listed below are the Deluxe resorts and the main details about each:

- *Animal Kingdom Lodge*
  - Phone-407-938-4799
  - Price Range-\$225-\$675
  - Closest Park-Animal Kingdom Lodge
  - Number of rooms-1,293
  - Room Size-Approximately 344 square feet

- Most rooms have two double beds or one bed and bunk beds
- Theme of Resort-African Savannah
- Food/Dining-Counter service & sit-down restaurants
- Pool-One large themed pool: The main pool is 11,000 square feet which features a waterslide and a children's pool.
- Arusha Savannah has an overlook area where guests can walk out and view the animals

- ***Beach Club & Yacht Club***
  - Phone-Beach Club 407-934-8000 Yacht Club 407-934-7000
  - Price Range-$325-$750
  - Closest Park-Epcot
  - Number of rooms-1,213 combined BC & YC
  - Room Size-Approximately 380 square feet
  - Most rooms have two double beds
  - Theme of Resort-New England Seashore
  - Food/Dining-Counter service & sit-down restaurants
  - Pool-One large themed pool and one small pool: The main pool is shared between Beach Club & Yacht Club, called Stormalong Bay, and features a waterslide that runs from the top of a stranded ship to the pool. This pool also features a lazy river and has a sand bottom. There is even a beach area for younger children. This is one of the top ranked resort pools in the world.
  - Walking entrance to Epcot's International Gateway
  - Short walk to Disney's Boardwalk area

- ***Boardwalk Inn***
  - Phone-407-939-5100
  - Price Range-$325-$790
  - Closest Park-Epcot
  - Number of rooms-378

- Room Size-Approximately 380 square feet
- Most rooms have two double beds
- Theme of Resort-Atlantic Seaside
- Food/Dining-Counter service & sit-down restaurants located on the Boardwalk
- Pool-One large themed pool and two small pools: The main pool is the Luna Park pool and features a waterslide called "Keister Coaster". The theme is a carnival setting. The two quiet pools serve the Disney Vacation Club (DVC) area and the garden courtyard area
- Walking entrance to Epcot's International Gateway
- Walking path to Disney's Hollywood Studios

- *Contemporary*
  - Phone-407-824-1000
  - Price Range-$270-$795
  - Closest Park-Magic Kingdom
  - Number of rooms-1,041
  - Room Size-Approximately 435 square feet
  - Most rooms have two double beds
  - Theme of Resort-Futuristic/Modern
  - Food/Dining-Counter service & sit-down restaurants
  - Pool-One large themed pool and one smaller pool: The main pool has a 17 foot high curving waterslide. The smaller quiet pool is shallow around the edges and deeper in the middle
  - Located on the monorail line to the Magic Kingdom

- *Grand Floridian*
  - Phone-407-824-3000
  - Price Range-$385-$990
  - Closest Park-Magic Kingdom
  - Number of rooms-900

- Room Size-Approximately 440 square feet
- Most rooms have two double beds
- Theme of Resort-Victorian
- Food/Dining-Counter service & sit-down restaurants
- Pool-One large themed pool and one courtyard pool: The main beachside pool features a waterslide and waterfall. The courtyard pool is more serene.
- Located on the monorail line to the Magic Kingdom

- *Polynesian*
  - Phone-407-824-3174
  - Price Range-$340-$860
  - Closest Park-Magic Kingdom
  - Number of rooms-853
  - Room Size-Approximately 410 square feet
  - Most rooms have two double beds
  - Theme of Resort-Tropical South Pacific
  - Food/Dining-Counter service & sit-down restaurants
  - Pool-One large themed pool and one smaller pool: The Nanea Volcano pool features a waterfall and a waterslide. The quieter, but larger pool is centrally located to all the longhouses.
  - Located on the monorail line to the Magic Kingdom

- *Wilderness Lodge*
  - Phone-407-824-3232
  - Price Range-$225-$730
  - Closest Park-Magic Kingdom
  - Number of rooms-728
  - Room Size-Approximately 340 square feet
  - Most rooms have two double beds
  - Theme of Resort-American National Park/Northwest US

- Food/Dining-Counter service & sit-down restaurants
- Pool-One large themed pool: The pool features a waterslide and the beginning of the pool is actually a bubbling geyser that runs outside to Silver Creek Falls and into the pool.

These resorts each have a different theme and each is close to a certain park. The Grand Floridian, Polynesian, and Contemporary are on the Magic Kingdom Monorail line. The Magic Kingdom is a short boat ride from The Wilderness Lodge. Boardwalk Inn, Beach Club, and Yacht Club are within walking distance of EPCOT and Disney's Hollywood Studios. Animal Kingdom and the Animal Kingdom Lodge are within minutes of each other. The Deluxe resorts are places where you can spend a significant amount of your day, so if you are planning on not spending the majority of your time in the parks, a deluxe resort may be the way to go. Cost could be a factor in your decision. The cost for deluxe rooms ranges from $225–$2100 depending on the room type, the season, and the view you want. It is always a good idea to check the Disney Web site well in advance to price out what the cost would be for various resorts for the dates of your trip.

Disney Vacation Club Resorts

Disney Vacation Club (DVC) resorts are very similar to the deluxe resorts except you can get one, two, or even three bedrooms at these resorts. These Villas can range in price depending on the type of room you choose and your vacation season. Listed below are the Disney Vacation Club resorts:

- *Animal Kingdom Lodge Villas*
  - Phone-407-824-3232
  - Price Range-$265-Unknown at present time
  - Number of rooms-458 units
  - Pool-One main pool: The Samawati Springs pool will be 4,700 square feet featuring a waterslide and two whirlpools. There will also be an interactive water area for children
  - Other information is same as Disney's Animal Kingdom Lodge
- *Beach Club Villas*
  - Phone-407-934-8000
  - Price Range-$325–$1,140

- Number of rooms-282 units
- Other information is same as Beach Club Resort

- **Boardwalk Villas**
  - Phone-407-939-5100
  - Price Range-$325-$2,125
  - Number of rooms-383 units
  - Other information is same as Boardwalk Inn Resort

- **Old Key West**
  - Phone-407-827-700
  - Price Range-$285-$1,645
  - Number of rooms-709 units
  - Theme-Key West Florida
  - Food/Dining-Counter service & Sit-down restaurant
  - Pool-One main pool and three small pools-The main pool has a waterslide and a kids' pool. The second pool is a bit smaller on Turtle Pond Road and features a snack bar. The other two quiet pools service the buildings in their area.

- **Saratoga Springs Resort and Spa**
  - Phone-407-827-1100
  - Price Range-$285-$1,645
  - Number of rooms-828 units
  - Theme-Upstate New York community
  - Food/Dining-Counter service & Sit-down restaurant
  - Pool-One main pool, one smaller pool and three quiet pools-The main pool is called High Rock Springs. It features a waterslide, a waterfall, and an interactive water play area. The newest pool is located in Grandstand area. There is also an interactive water feature at this pool. There are also three quiet pools servicing various buildings.

- **Villas at Wilderness Lodge**

- Phone-407-824-3232

- Price Range-$315-$1,120

- Number of rooms-181 units

- Other information is same as Disney's Wilderness Lodge

Other Disney Vacation Club locations are found in Hilton Head, South Carolina, Vero Beach, Florida, Hawaii, and at Disney's Grand Californian Resort in Anaheim, California. Disney Vacation Club resorts offer studio rooms which are comparable to the deluxe rooms as well as the larger suites. They offer the same type of amenities as deluxe resorts, with the addition of full-service kitchens and in-room laundry facilities for the one, two, or three bed-room suites. The price range again is between $265–$2155 per night.

Fort Wilderness Resort & Campground

One other type of resort is Disney's Fort Wilderness Campground. This campground is located near Wilderness Lodge and between Magic Kingdom and Epcot. You have the option to stay outside on the campground or inside a cabin.

- **Fort Wilderness Resort & Campground**

  - Phone-407-824-2900

  - Price Range-$35 (campsite)-$275 (cabin)

  - Number of rooms-409 cabins

  - Theme-Wilderness/Settlement

  - Food/Dining-Counter service & Sit-down restaurant

  - Pool-One main pool and one smaller pool: The main pool is located near the Meadow Trading Post in the center of the campground. The second pool is located near the Wilderness Cabins, closer to the resort entrance.

WDW Peak Season Advice

Do:

- Stay "On-Property"

- Decide what you can afford

- Figure out how much time you will be in your room

- Research to see what type of theme resort best fits the needs of your family

- **Make your resort reservation as early as possible**. You only need to pay one night's deposit when you make the reservation, and it will be refunded if you cancel outside of 5 days prior to arrival. It is best to make your reservation way in advance for the resort, room type and view while you can. You can always change it later.

- Take advantage of all the benefits of staying "On-Property"

Don't:

- Wait until a few months before your trip to pick your resort. You may be disappointed to know that the resort, room type, or view you wanted is unavailable.

4

Making the most of your time at the Parks

In order to maximize your time at the parks, you must begin your strategy first thing in the morning. **Get to the parks early**! If you do not adhere to this, your trip will be set up for disappointment right from the beginning. Most books have touring plans and such, but the majority of these plans will not work during the peak seasons. Some offer the "commando style" touring approach that, unless you are a marathon runner, have no kids, or don't care to actually enjoy Disney, work just fine. Who wants to have to race from ride to ride or stick to a strict schedule while on vacation?

The problem that I have found with these plans is that they make people slaves to them, no matter how "flexible" they say they are. Peak seasons are an entirely different animal to conquer when touring the parks. People should not have to look at their "touring plan" and think to themselves, "Boy we need to hurry up to get to #6 on our list". These plans do not work because they forget some of the key issues during peak seasons.... more people = more unexpected problems. What happens to your plan when a ride like Test Track breaks down and you get stuck on it, or you are waiting in line for over an hour as they try to fix the ride? What happens to your plan when a ride you have a FASTPASS for has a line backed up because earlier in the day the ride was shut down? Now everyone who had a FASTPASS return time earlier than yours is ahead of you in line. Your FASTPASS is now a "SLOWPASS that is wasting my touring time." What happens to your plan when it begins to rain and everyone rushes into Mickey's Star Traders to buy a poncho and there is only one Cast Member working? Your touring plan just isn't going to work.

If you are tied to a touring plan, especially during peak seasons, your vacation frustration will soon settle in. As a result you then begin to deviate from any plan and everyone becomes frustrated. What happens when it takes you fifteen more

47

minutes than you planned because you cannot get through Fantasyland in the afternoon because strollers block most walking areas between Mickey's Philharmagic to Cinderella's Golden Carousel? What happens when the wait times for Peter Pan, Space Mountain, or Splash Mountain are at 240 minutes each and you have wasted a FASTPASS on Stitch's Great Escape earlier? These are issues you have to consider.

Maybe the biggest obstacle that touring plans don't factor in is the "tour groups". These large amounts of teenage tour groups from South America converge on Walt Disney World mainly in the summertime. They are usually accompanied by a few adults, but it never seems to be enough. The purpose here though isn't to complain about the tour groups, but to point out a few complications that will ruin those touring plans that are out there. What happens when as your touring plan says to ride Soarin' next, and as you enter the Land pavilion and make your way downstairs, you encounter hundreds of teenagers from a tour group in front of you? Unless you have a FASTPASS you are left with two choices, wait in an extended line (200+ minutes), or waste more time by walking to another attraction. What happens when your touring plan tells you to eat lunch at a certain time? However, as you enter the restaurant you chose, you encounter a tour group filling up each line. Your choice is to leave and go to another restaurant, (which may have another tour group there) or just stay in line. Either choice will affect your touring plan negatively.

These are only a few of the many examples that can kill even the most "flexible" of touring plans out there. That is why in this book we won't give you specific touring plans. They don't work during peak seasons. We will give you suggestions, ideas, and tips that we have tested and have worked for us during the peak seasons. I am not saying just show up and go with the flow because that will not work. You really need some general tips and advice. I challenge anyone to follow another book's touring plan during peak season, and then follow some of the suggestions I provide. My guess is that those who try my methods will have a much better Disney experience than following a plan that is set up to fail, or frustrate you, if things don't go just right.

Let's focus on getting to the actual parks. With my wife and I being teachers we can only travel during the peak seasons, and we continue to have wonderful vacations. We know what works and what doesn't, as we experience these seasons every year. We will not necessarily give you "touring plans," but strategies that will help make the most of your vacation.

First of all, be aware that Spring Break, summer, and the Christmas holiday season are the most crowded Walt Disney World will ever be. The reason is that most kids are not in school and Walt Disney World makes for a great family destination. The negative with that is that it seems like *every* family in the world has the same plans. Without proper planning you are setting yourself up for major frustration during your vacation.

Get to the parks early. Get to the parks early. We cannot stress that enough. Utilize Extra Magic Hours (EMH) in the morning. There are some plans that say to avoid EMH because that is where everyone is going. We say if you can get up and get any rides/shows completed in the first hour, you should do it. We have found that many people will sleep in and then arrive at the parks about 10:00 AM or 10:30 AM. You should have something quick for breakfast on the go. Bring something like a breakfast bar, Pop Tart etc … to eat on the ride to the park. Get your coffee in a to-go cup and head toward the buses. This should be enough to tide everyone over for a few hours. Don't waste precious park touring time eating a sit-down breakfast at your resort. This is one of the mistakes many people make. When they arrive at the parks about an hour or two after it is open, they cannot believe how crowded it is. During peak seasons, you have to adjust and try to only eat in the resort for breakfast once or twice. Otherwise you will be getting to the parks with a thousand of your (not) best friends and the frustration will begin to mount. Another option is to make a breakfast reservation at a restaurant that is inside one of the parks, at a time listed *before* the park opens. If you make a reservation at one of those restaurants (they usually open about an hour before the park opens) you can enter the park an hour early and eat. If you can finish eating before the park officially opens you are already ahead of the rest of the pack who are still waiting at the turnstiles. Please note that even though you are technically in the park before it opens, you do not have access to certain parts of the park. There are ropes that block off that access. You do indeed get to advance farther than everyone else.

E-Ticket rides are the top rides in each park. They are termed that based on an old ticket system that Disney used to use to place a value on each ride. For example the least thrilling ride was deemed an A-Ticket. Working their way up a B-Ticket was an attraction that offered a little more for visitors. E-Ticket was the highest ranking ride. So when we refer to E-Ticket rides we are talking about the E-Ticket or best rides/attractions found at Walt Disney World.

On days when EMH mornings are offered, you should get to that park by opening and ride some E-Ticket rides before the park opens to everyone an hour later. Most of the rides available for EMH are E-Ticket rides, so it is always good to get them done as soon as possible. Then when the park opens to everyone, it will become crowded very quickly. The advantage you have is you have completed several of the key E-Ticket rides already and can now focus on other attractions. By about noon or 1:00 PM, you can leave the park. Go back to your room and relax, or go for a swim. This is the time of the day when all the slackers (those who sleep in) arrive at the parks. The parks will be packed and on certain days, may even be at capacity. Late comers may have to return to the resort. The parks "close" because of the enormous crowds. We have witnessed this at the water parks as well. While the late-comers are all frustrated and waiting in lines, you are relaxing at your resort or the pool.

As those late arrivals are leaving in the evening, you can go back to the parks. Will it still be crowded? You bet! This is the peak season at Walt Disney World. You will have already enjoyed many rides, gotten a swim in, and maybe even napped. Now you are refreshed as you re-enter the park at night. You can use the nighttime to focus on shows, rides that maybe are not the most popular, eat a snack or dinner, and spend some time shopping. By using this strategy you can maximize your touring of the parks. We cannot stress enough though that you should not plan on doing many of the E-Ticket rides in the evening during these times. The exception is to head over to the popular rides *during* the parade or fireworks. If you have never seen the parade or fireworks show then disregard this advice as you should always see them at least once. If you have seen them and are intent on doing the top rides in the evening, this is the time to try to hit those rides. Some rides like Big Thunder Mountain Railroad are completely different in the dark. One of our best and most memorable Jungle Cruise adventures was during "Wishes," the nighttime fireworks show. We all love the Tomorrowland Transit Authority (People-Mover) after dark. Watching "Spectromagic" from above is amazing.

WDW Peak Season Advice

Do:

- **Get up early and get to the parks!**
- Utilize EMH if available in the AM
- Keep it simple. Ride early and often at your favorite rides, then leave 3-4 hours later.
- Eat something light and on the go on your way to the parks

- If you must eat a big breakfast, make a reservation at a restaurant inside the park at the earliest time they offer. Check the time the park is supposed to open that day and make your reservation about one hour earlier than that if available.

- Go back to the resort in the afternoon to swim or relax when everyone else is entering the parks.

- Try to obtain a FASTPASS for an E-Ticket ride BEFORE you leave to go back to the resort in the afternoon. The return time may be for later that evening.

- Return to the park in the evening when others are leaving

- Try to do rides that aren't the most popular, or go to shows that others might overlook

- View the second parade of the evening if it is offered.

- **Get up early and get to the parks**!

Don't:

- Sleep in. You will only put yourself behind for the day.

- Think you will be able to just walk onto any rides. If you get to the parks about an hour and a half or so after it opens, FASTPASSES may be gone, lines will be building, and the park will be packed.

- Stay all day long! You will be tired, your kids will be tired, and if touring in the summer, everyone will be hot and miserable. Don't make that mistake.

- Expect to return at night and get on rides. The lines will be filled with people who have waited at least an hour to ride the more popular rides.

- Fight to see the first parade of the evening if they offer two parades. Many people will leave after the first parade and fireworks show.

FASTPASS

What is FASTPASS you may ask? It is a ticket that will allow you quicker access on many of the top rides with minimal wait in line. Since this book is geared toward people who have to travel around school vacations, let me put it in terms that our kids will understand. Basically you get to cut most people in line!

Most of the E-Ticket rides in Walt Disney World have FASTPASS machines next to the ride entrance. Look for the sign that says FASTPASS Distribution. This is where you want to go. When you get there you place your Walt Disney World park ticket in the slot and out will come a FASTPASS. The FASTPASS will have a designated time listed for you to come back to ride the attraction. When you return during this time frame you will then look to the other side of the ride entrance for a sign that says FASTPASS Return. Walk up to the Cast Member and show them the FASTPASS. You will walk through a different line than the regular people (cutting most of them). This will allow you minimal wait time.

What happens if you are late arriving for the ride and it is AFTER the listed time frame? Don't worry, most Cast Members are instructed to allow the FAST-PASS to still be honored. They understand that things can happen and you may be late. This is not guaranteed, but we have never had a problem using a FAST-PASS shortly after the time had expired.

It sounds like you can just walk up to every ride that offers FASTPASS and get one for that ride, right? Wrong. This is Disney and they want you to have some time to be able to spend your money at a gift shop or restaurant. What Disney has done is implement a system where you can only get a valid FASTPASS every so often. When you get your first FASTPASS of the day it will give you a return time printed on it. Let's say it is 9:30 AM and you go to Space Mountain to get a FASTPASS for later. You put your park ticket in the machine and it gives you a FASTPASS that may look like this: "Return anytime between 10:10 AM and 11:10 AM".

From this point on it is a good idea to go on rides that do not offer FAST-PASSES because you will have to wait a bit in a line at some point on your trip. Our goal is to maximize your touring of the parks. So you might as well wait in line at a ride that *doesn't* have FASTPASS. Another plus for doing this after you have gotten a FASTPASS, is while you are waiting in line, you will be getting another ride out of the way, as well as inching closer to your FASTPASS return time. Make sure you do this method throughout the day! *If by some chance you are at a park early enough and you notice there is a short line or minimal wait time for a FASTPASS offered attraction, by all means go ahead and ride it.*

You can then go on another ride or two and when you are finished with those, walk back to Space Mountain, enter through the FASTPASS line anytime between 10:10 AM and 11:10 AM, and get on the ride. You ask, "When can I get another FASTPASS then?" Well the times will vary, but this information will be printed on the bottom of the FASTPASS ticket you get. If you got your first

FASTPASS for Space Mountain at 9:30 AM you may be able to get another one around 10:10 AM or 10:15 AM. Disney is always changing the exact way you can obtain another FASTPASS so just make sure you check the bottom of your FASTPASS.

The Runner

When you are able to get another FASTPASS you should go to another place in the park and obtain another FASTPASS for later use. A variation of this calls for someone in your group to be a "runner". What that means is since you are touring the parks during peak season most rides will be packed and FASTPASSES will be gone early in the day. So to maximize your day, have one person in your group collect everyone's park tickets and walk/run to another area of the park and obtain FASTPASSES for everyone in the group to use later in the day. Yes, this is allowed. By using a "runner" your entire group doesn't have to walk to another part of the park to get FASTPASSES, and then return back to where they were. If you want to maximize your time, have the "runner" go get those FASTPASSES when everyone else goes to the restroom or goes to get a drink or something. By doing this, you will not inconvenience others in your group and later in the day they will all be appreciative of your effort to go get those FASTPASSES.

One other trick is to obtain a FASTPASS BEFORE you get onto the ride, save that FASTPASS for later, and immediately enter the stand-by line of the ride. When you exit the ride there is a good change that your FASTPASS time will be ready and you can go right on the attraction again.

Another option to maximize your ability to possibly hit some top rides in the evening is to get FASTPASSES BEFORE you leave the park in the afternoon. Many times during the peak seasons FASTPASSES are all distributed by early afternoon. For example, if you are planning on leaving Magic Kingdom at 1:00 PM, you may want to stop by Space Mountain right before you leave. Many times FASTPASSES will be available for later on in the evening. You may get lucky and can get FASTPASSES for something like a return time of 9:00-10:00 PM. Take them back to the resort, and then you will have FASTPASSES for at least one ride later that night when you return.

We do not get into specific touring plans because when you are touring during peak seasons, all bets are off. Our recommendation is as follows:

Use FASTPASS for the following rides. After you have ridden those, time permitting, you can obtain FASTPASSES for the other secondary rides if needed. You should not get a FASTPASS for one of the secondary rides if you haven't ridden all the top ones first.

Animal Kingdom

- Use FASTPASS for these "E-Ticket" rides: *Expedition Everest, Kilimanjaro Safari, Kali River Rapids*

- Do NOT use FASTPASS for these secondary rides until you have ridden the E-Ticket rides first: *It's Tough to be a Bug, Dinosaur, Primeval Whirl*

When you enter it is a good idea to go straight toward Expedition Everest. I know that's where everyone else is going, but you have to do it. Even if you have to wait just a bit here in the morning you will have gotten the #1 ride out of the way. You have the option to obtain a FASTPASS for Expedition Everest then head to Kilimanjaro Safari and use the stand-by line. The wait in the morning should be minimal. After you ride that, you can head back to Expedition Everest and use your FASTPASS. You can then head to Kali River Rapids after Expedition Everest. As long as you know which rides to potentially FASTPASS and which not to, you should be ok.

Epcot

- Use FASTPASS for these "E-Ticket" rides: *Soarin', Test Track, Mission Space*

- Do NOT use FASTPASS for these secondary rides until you have ridden the E-Ticket rides first: *Maelstrom, Honey I Shrunk the Audience, Living with the Land*

This is the park where once you enter you make a choice to either go right toward Soarin' or left towards Mission Space and Test Track. It is a good idea here to use the "runner". Have someone make the trek over to Soarin' and get FASTPASSES for your group to use later. Everyone can walk toward Test Track and Mission Space. When the runner returns, go to the stand-by line for either Test Track or Mission Space and ride that attraction. Then go to the other ride immediately afterward. By that time the FASTPASS window should be available and have the group head toward Soarin'. Use your FASTPASS for this attraction and within an hour or so you will have accomplished the top three rides in Epcot.

Disney's Hollywood Studios

- Use FASTPASS for these "E-Ticket" rides: *Rock N' Rollercoaster, Tower of Terror*

- Do NOT use FASTPASS for these secondary rides until you have ridden the E-Ticket rides first: *Star Tours, Voyage of the Little Mermaid, Lights Motors Action Extreme Stunt Show, Indiana Jones*

These two are in the same area so *everyone* will head to them. That is ok. Pick one of the two and get a FASTPASS for it. Then go ride the other attraction. When you finish that ride use your FASTPASS.

Magic Kingdom

- Use FASTPASS for these "E-Ticket" rides: *Space Mountain, Big Thunder Mountain Railroad, Splash Mountain, Peter Pan*

- Do NOT use FASTPASS for these secondary rides until you have ridden the E-Ticket rides first: *Stitch's Great Escape, Mickey's Philharmagic, Jungle Cruise, Buzz Lightyear, Adventures of Winnie the Pooh*

Magic Kingdom is much harder to utilize FASTPASSES because it will almost definitely require a "runner" if you want to maximize your time and make the touring of the park enjoyable and hassle free. There are so many different variations on which ride to FASTPASS first. What we want to focus on is deciding which direction you are going to go when you enter the park. If you are going toward Frontierland, have your runner go the opposite side and get FAST-PASSES for everyone for Space Mountain. That way you can tour the park from the left around to the right and end up at Space Mountain. If you can go toward Space Mountain first then have your runner go get a FASTPASS for something on the opposite side of the park, such as Splash Mountain. The third option is to just go one way or the other and obtain a FASTPASS for your E-Ticket ride on that side, go on the ride and then just return later on during your designated time frame.

Another Option for Magic Kingdom is to devote two days toward that park. On your first day, start on Main Street U.S.A. and work your way one direction. On the second day go in the opposite direction. If you have little ones, you may want to head straight to Fantasyland first instead of right or left.

WDW Peak Season Advice

Do:

• Utilize FASTPASS

• Have a "runner" to go get FASTPASSES for the family or group to use later in the day

• Obtain another FASTPASS as soon as the printed time says you can

• Get a FASTPASS and then go to rides that do NOT have FASTPASS. You will have to wait in some lines, so at least make them for rides that do NOT offer FASTPASS to get them out of the way.

• Use FASTPASS for secondary attractions AFTER you have done the E-Ticket attractions

• Try to get a FASTPASS for a ride before you go to lunch. That way you may be able to make useful time while waiting for the FASTPASS return time.

• View a show while you are waiting for your FASTPASS return time to come around.

Don't:

• Wait in lines for rides that offer FASTPASS (only as a last resort or unless you want to do the ride 2-3 times in a row)

• Waste a FASTPASS for a secondary ride until you have finished the E-Ticket rides

• Drag your entire family from one side of the park to the other just to obtain FASTPASSES for use later in the day

• Make the mistake of not planning your touring route without using FAST-PASSES. Keep in mind you are traveling during Peak season, so it will be packed.

• Expect to do every ride with minimal wait without using FASTPASS

• Expect FASTPASSES for the E-Ticket rides to be available after 2:00-3:00 PM. These are usually gone before noon on some days.

- Use FASTPASS during morning EMH. You won't be able to use them until after the park opens to regular guests, so just save the option until later.

Another key is to know which rides to NOT FASTPASS. I am sure you are wondering why we say to not waste FASTPASSES for certain rides. First, many rides will take care of themselves if you get to the parks early, especially with EMH's. You can really knock out quite a few rides in the first hour if you use EMH in the morning. Even if there aren't EMH in the morning, you can still ride many of the top rides in the first hour. We have been able to do every ride in Fantasyland, some twice, in about an hour during EMH. It's usually about two hours into the park opening that the parks start to fill up.

At Animal Kingdom, rides that offer FASTPASS, but you shouldn't use are It's Tough to be a Bug, and Dinosaur. For ITTBAB, you do not need to use a FASTPASS. This attraction sometimes is forgotten by many as it sits in the Tree of Life and many people just walk right by it going toward Kilimanjaro Safari or Expedition Everest. Dinosaur is a tough one because there are times when you may need to use a FASTPASS for it, but as long as you can get the E-Ticket rides out of the way early, most visitors can usually handle a twenty minute wait for it. For Primeval Whirl, a FASTPASS could be used once you have ridden the E-Ticket rides. Check the wait time on the way to Expedition Everest or Kali River Rapids then decide.

In Epcot, there are a few rides that are not worth burning a FASTPASS on. Maelstrom in Norway is one of them. Many people don't even ride the attraction so the lines are usually short. Another ride is Honey I Shrunk the Audience. This theatre seats plenty and the wait time for it usually is about twenty minutes. Compare that to Soarin' which can have a wait time reaching toward 120 minutes. The other ride is Living with the Land. This one can be deceiving. Many times people will get FASTPASSES for Soarin' and just walk right over and ride Living with the Land. But don't be fooled. If the line is long come back later and chances are it won't be. All we can say about this ride is if you miss it, you will survive. If gardening is your thing, go for it.

Disney's Hollywood Studios offers a few rides that fall into our category. Outside of Star Wars Weekends, Star Tours doesn't seem to have a wait time longer than twenty minutes. If you time it wrong, you may wind up heading to the line right as the Indiana Jones stunt show has ended. The wait time may jump because of hundreds of people heading the same direction after the show. Lights Motors Action and Indiana Jones fall into the category of huge facilities to accommodate thousands. Don't waste your FASTPASS option here. While these shows do pack them in, it seems that people always seem to get find a seat. A better use of your FASTPASS is to obtain ANOTHER FASTPASS for Rock N' Rollercoaster or Tower of Terror and use it later in the day.

Magic Kingdom again has the most options. While we say do not use FAST-PASS for secondary rides, Magic Kingdom is the one place that you may have to. Just remember to ride all the E-Ticket rides *first* using FASTPASS, then you can go for the secondary attractions. Buzz Lightyear's Space Ranger Spin is the one ride where you may consider using a FASTPASS after you have done all the "E-Ticket" attractions. This one occasionally will have longer lines later in the day. The Many Adventures of Winnie the Pooh falls into the same category as Buzz Lightyear. I would use a FASTPASS for this ride only after you have done the E-Ticket rides. Mickey's Philharmagic seats plenty and your wait time for it is usually only one show, so about 20 minutes. Jungle Cruise is hit or miss. We have seen its wait times approach 60-70 minutes and other times during peak seasons the wait is twenty minutes. File this with Pooh and Buzz as good secondary rides. As for Stitch's Great Escape, if you like something that scares children, grosses out adults, and overall just wastes about thirty minutes, go ahead and do it.

WDW Peak Season Advice

Do:

• Use FASTPASS for secondary rides *only after* you have first used them up for the top attractions

Don't:

• Waste a FASTPASS on a secondary ride until you have done the top attractions first

• Get a FASTPASS during EMH's

Rider Switch

What is a Rider Switch? Rider Switch is an option that can be utilized to save time and headaches for families. What a rider switch does is allow for one parent to go on a ride while the other waits with the child. As soon as the first parent gets off the ride, they "switch" and the second parent can ride the attraction without having to walk through the line again. This also works when you have multiple children and only one child is tall enough to ride the attraction.

Preparation

We must stress that you do need a general plan in the parks, but do not just focus on an exact plan. The fun of Disney is also being spontaneous and taking in some of the little things that may make your vacation memorable.

Our first piece of advice is to have a plan of how you want to tour the parks *before* you get there. There are many places on the web that offer park maps to view. You can even call Disney and ask them to send you park maps. Have an idea beforehand of what type of rides you or the kids will enjoy and which they will not. If you aren't sure, here's a tip.... **ask them**! Sure, they may not know exactly the details of each ride, but if you have a map with you or are looking at a website, you can read the description to them. That will give them a better idea of that ride. Remember that if this is a family vacation, you want to give your kids some input as well in order to make a smoother trip for everyone. We are not here to tell you which rides to do. That is up to you to decide. After all, some of us like big thrills, some of us like spinning, and some of us just like to meander and take in the sights. Many people make the mistake of never even preparing. They grab a map when they enter the park and then try to figure out which direction to go. We have even heard someone ask a Cast Member, "What rides do you have here?" Preparation is the key. Spending a little time researching this before you go will definitely pay off when you arrive at the parks.

Another good idea after you have done a little research would be for you to find out the specifications for each ride. How tall do you have to be to ride it? Are there any special warnings involved with the ride? This can also help you plan attractions you will be able to do as a family, or if it is something you would enjoy at all.

You now have some background about what FASTPASS rides are in each park, which attractions you can ride, and which rides/shows you may have an interest in doing. If you have prepared ahead of time you should have a general idea of where the E-Ticket rides are situated in each park. That will give you a better understanding of which direction you want to tour the park. Again everyone is different so pick the way that best suits the needs and interests of your family. Make sure though to hit the E-Ticket rides first, and go from there. It should be advised that you may want to get a FASTPASS for an E-Ticket ride and while you are waiting for your return time to come up, enjoy a show like *Finding Nemo the Musical* instead of a ride. Remember you are here during a peak season and you don't want to waste valuable touring time trying to figure out where you are going and what to do.

A good tip is to pick up a park map in the lobby of your resort before you get on the bus. They have them for every park, so grab a map and get acquainted with it on the bus. This is good two ways. One it allows you time to figure out your touring plan for the day. Two, if you get maps for the kids as well, it occupies their time on the bus and even allows them to get excited about which rides they want to do. It is also a good idea to pick up park maps as you leave your first park for the day. That will allow you some time in your resort room to fine-tune your plan for the next day. If you forget to do that, just go to the lobby when you return to your resort and pick up another one. *As a side note, when you check into your Disney resort you do get a packet of information that usually contains all the park maps.*

WDW Peak Season Advice

Do:

- Plan ahead of time. Order park maps from Disney or research them on the Internet

- Get input from your kids. Discuss with your kids rides that sound fun to them

- Figure out the restrictions for each ride you may want to go on

- Grab a map from your lobby before you get to the park. Look it over on the bus ride from your resort.

- Ride the E-Ticket rides first and tour the parks accordingly after that

- Take some time to enjoy the little things that Disney offers.

Don't:

- Just show up at Walt Disney World having no idea about any rides to go on

- Ignore rides that your kids may want to go on

- Wait in line for a long time, then when you finally get up to entering the ride, finally realize that there are restrictions that will prevent you from getting on

- Assume that you will be able to just walk up to whatever ride you want and get right on. This is a peak season and you need a plan. The lines will be long so adjust accordingly.

- Tour "commando style" where you just race from place to place. If you have a plan stick as close to it as possible, but allow for some time to just enjoy Disney

EMH

Extra Magic Hours at each park are a bit different. EMH mornings allow one park to open an hour earlier in the morning and EMH evening allows a park to stay open three hours later. Each park will offer different rides to be open during these times. It is important to know which attractions will be available during these times. Again it is our preference to advise people to utilize EMH, especially the morning ones. This is contradictory to what many other books say. They say that that park will be overrun with people, and to choose another park. What we have found is that during peak seasons *every park* is packed. You are better off to get up early and utilize that first hour if at all possible. The EMH park does become more crowded as the day wears on. However, you can get several E-ticket attractions out of the way in that first hour. By getting there at opening on an EMH day, we have been able to ride, Buzz Lightyear, Space Mountain, Tomorrowland Indy Speedway, Mad Tea Party, Many Adventures of Winnie the Pooh, Snow White, Cinderella's Golden Carousel, and It's a Small World all before 9:00 AM. It really is worth it. Mickey will even give On-Site guests a wake-up call to get you going on those early mornings.

What about the parades?

Ok, this is one of the biggest questions people have during the peak seasons. Our advice is if you have never seen any Walt Disney World parade then yes, you should attend them. If you have seen them before then our advice is the skip them and utilize that time to ride some of the more popular rides, as many people will lineup to watch the parades. Let's break down the different parades:

Magic Kingdom offers an afternoon parade as well as a nighttime parade. Epcot offers no parades, while Animal Kingdom offers an afternoon parade, and Disney's Hollywood Studios also offers an afternoon parade. During the peak seasons, many times Magic Kingdom will offer two afternoon parades and two nighttime parades. If Magic Kingdom offers two afternoon parades, you should try to view the first one, only because you should be getting ready to exit the parks about this time (1:00 PM). Take advantage of this and stay to watch the first parade and leave right after to get back to the resort to swim or relax. If there is only one parade scheduled for the afternoon, then your choice is either get to a spot early (about forty-five minutes ahead of time) or by-pass the parades and go on rides. If you must view the parades, keep in mind that there will always be the late comers who try to rush right in front of you, or who huddle up behind you and force their kids past you so they can be in the front. Our advice is to have a towel, poncho or something to "mark your territory". If you are with your family they should fill up that space. Try your best to hold your ground. When watching parades during peak seasons it resembles an all out battle of wills, to see who can flex their muscles and stand their ground. Be prepared to fight off others, but in a Disney friendly way of course. Another tip if you have a stroller, find a place near a pole or somewhere where the stroller can be a blockade at one end of your group so no one can come past from that way. If you have never toured during peak season, these are things you have to do to insure a quality viewing for yourself, family and kids. Don't be surprised if you end up getting aced out of that perfect spot you found on Main Street USA.

The Magic Kingdom many times will offer its nighttime parade, *Spectromagic*, twice during the evening. If that is the case, then you should try to stay and view the second parade. Sure, you will be required to stay up later, but trust us it is well worth it. Many people will either leave after the first parade or after *Wishes*, the fireworks show. You can go on rides during the first parade then watch the fireworks. As people are fighting to rush out to the buses, monorail, or ferry you can enjoy a soda or ice-cream and wait for the second parade with much less hassle. Make sure you stay in the park after the second parade. Let others rush out in a stampede. This is the time to go into the shops for any last minute merchandise or popcorn for the road. Then, head for the bus stop. You will be very relaxed, all things considered.

Viewing areas for parades vary, but in general here are a few tips. First and foremost, if you are attempting to view a parade during a peak season you must get to a spot at least forty-five minutes before hand and claim your location. You also must stay there otherwise there will always be someone who budges their way into your territory anyway. Next, get as close to the rope as you can and that way there is no room for anyone to jump in front of you at the last minute. In fact, sit with your legs out past the rope, then as the parade nears you can pull them in.

In the Magic Kingdom, try to avoid Main Street USA. I know that this is the prettiest viewing area, but everyone wants to be there, so there are a lot of late comers who can ruin your parade viewing experience. Again we speak from past experience. Unfortunately, people are rude and will push their way right in front of the spot you picked out forty-five minutes earlier, and they won't feel bad about doing it. So to ease a little of the parade pressure in Magic Kingdom, find another spot. You can usually find a good spot in Frontierland on either side of the parade path.

In Animal Kingdom the parade route travels past the Africa section in the beginning and also at the end of the route. You can find a place there and see it twice. If you get there late, many people will leave after the parade starts, then you can find a place to sit and just wait for it to come around the park back toward you.

In Disney's Hollywood Studios, if you look closely on the ground you may see areas that have some silver lines embedded into the ground. Those are areas where the parade will come past and areas where ropes are placed. If you can find areas where two lines meet and make an angle, position your family right there and no one will be able to get in front of you. The silver boundaries in the ground basically block you off from others. Now I cannot tell you exactly where these parts are. We want to give you something to look for. Just don't try to get in front of us if we get there first.

WDW Peak Season Advice

Do:

• Get to a spot about forty-five minutes early if you must view a parade

• View the second parade at Magic Kingdom if it is offered

• Have something to "mark your territory" with such as a towel or poncho

• Sit as close to a rope as possible with your feet extended out in front of you. Remember as the parade approaches you can always pull your legs and feet back in

• Be prepared to stand your ground

• Walk through the shops if you stayed for the second nighttime parade at Magic Kingdom while everyone else battles toward the buses

Don't:

• Expect to walk right up and find a good spot five minutes before the parade starts

• Think people won't try to push their way in front of you and your family

- Give anyone room to wiggle in front of you and your family

- Rush out to the buses if you stayed for the second nighttime parade at Magic Kingdom

Now that you have an understanding of the various methods that can make your trip to the parks a much better experience, let's focus on the rides/attractions at each park. We have attempted to give you a brief overview of every ride/show in each park. If any of the rides/shows use FASTPASS that will be listed as well as any height requirements. As far as the age appropriateness of each ride, we have listed a recommended age. These are more like guidelines than rules because every child, family, and pirate is different.

Magic Kingdom: Rides/Attractions/Shows

Adventureland

Name	Type	FASTPASS Available	Min. Height	Ages	Description
Enchanted Tiki Room	Show	No		2+	Audio-Animatronics bird show
Jungle Cruise	Ride	Yes		2+	Zany, humorous boat tour
Magic Carpets of Aladdin	Ride	No		2+	Fly over Agrabah on a magic carpet
Pirates of the Caribbean	Ride	No		3+	Dark ride featuring Captain Jack Sparrow and an array of pirate scenes
Swiss Family Treehouse	Walk	No		3+	A walk through tour of the Robinson's Treehouse

Fantasyland

Name	Type	FASTPASS Available	Min. Height	Ages	Description
Ariel's Grotto	Meet	No		1+	Meet and Greet with Ariel
Cinderella's Golden Carousel	Ride	No		2+	Ride Cinderella's Carousel and see if you can find her horse
Dream Along with Mickey	Show	No		1+	Castle Forecourt Stage—Mickey & Friends
Dumbo the Flying Elephant	Ride	No		2+	Soar over Fantasyland with Dumbo
it's a small world	Ride	No		1+	Musical indoor ride around the world
Mad Tea Party	Ride	No		3+	Spinning ride in a tea cup
Many Adventures of Winnie the Pooh	Ride	Yes		1+	Bounce, roll, and float through indoor adventures (sometimes dark)
Mickey's Philharmagic	Show	Yes		2+	3-D Adventure featuring Donald, Mickey and other Disney Characters
Peter Pan's Flight	Ride	Yes		3+	Dark Ride—Indoor flying adventure
Pooh's Playful Spot	Play	No		1+	Outdoor Play Area

Snow White's Scary Adventures	Ride	No	c	5+	Ride through the story of Snow White and the witch. *Dark Ride that can be scary for younger children*
Storytime with Belle	Show	No		1+	Fairytale Garden—Come join Belle as she tells the story of Beauty & the Beast

Frontierland

Name	Type	FASTPASS Available	Min. Height	Ages	Description
Big Thunder Mountain Railroad	Ride	Yes	40"		Runaway train rollercoaster
Country Bear Jamboree	Show	No		2+	Audio-Animatronics singing bear show
Splash Mountain	Ride	Yes	40"		Water Ride—Plunge five stories in Brer Rabbit's Laughin' Place
Tom Sawyer Island	Walk	No		2+	Explore the island—walking tour

Liberty Square

Name	Type	FASTPASS Available	Min. Height	Ages	Description
Hall of Presidents	Show	No		2+	Presidential audio-animatronics show
Haunted Mansion	Ride	No		5+	*Dark Ride that can be scary for younger children*
Liberty Square Riverboat	Ride	No		1+	Journey around Tom Sawyer's Island in a riverboat

Main Street USA

Name	Type	FASTPASS Available	Min. Height	Ages	Description
Disney Dreams Come True	Parade	No		1+	Afternoon parade featuring Disney Characters
Flag Retreat	Show	No		1+	In Town Square—Come watch as the ceremony as the flag is taken down for the day
Spectromagic	Parade	No		1+	Nighttime parade featuring Disney Characters
Walt Disney World Railroad	Ride	No		1+	Twenty minute roundtrip tour around the Magic Kingdom

| Wishes | Show | No | | 1+ | Nighttime fire-works show over Cinderella Castle |

Mickey's Toontown Fair

Name	Type	FASTPASS Available	Min. Height	Ages	Description
Barnstormer @ Goofy's Wise-acre Farm	Ride	No	35"		Crazy kiddie roll-ercoaster star-ring Goofy
Donald's Boat	Play	No		1+	Water play area
Judge's Tent	Meet	No		1+	Meet Mickey Mouse
Mickey's Coun-try House	Walk	No		1+	Walk thru Mickey's home
Minnie's Coun-try House	Walk	No		1+	Walk thru Min-nie's home
Toontown Hall of Fame	Meet	No		1+	Meet & Greet various Disney Characters

Tomorrowland

Name	Type	FASTPASS Available	Min. Height	Ages	Description
Astro Orbiter	Ride	No		5+	Fly outdoors in a spaceship over-looking the Magic Kingdom—*Can be scary for younger children*

Buzz Light-year's Space Ranger Spin	Ride	Yes		3+	Intergalactic interactive adventure as you try to accumu-late points and capture Zurg
Monsters Inc. Laugh Floor	Show	No		1+	Interactive com-edy show featur-ing monsters from Monstropo-lis
Space Moun-tain	Ride	Yes	44"		Dark Ride—Indoor rollercoaster through outer space.
Stitch's Great Escape!	Show	Yes	40"	5+	Interactive alien experience. *Dark Show that can be scary for younger children.*
Tomorrowland Indy Speedway	Ride	No	52" to ride alone	2+	Drive a race car around Tomor-rowland
Tomorrowland Transit Author-ity	Ride	No		2+	Roll through Tomorrowland with a bird's eye view
Walt Disney's Carousel of Progress	Show	No		2+	Audio-Animatron-ics show through time

Animal Kingdom: Rides/Attractions/Shows

Africa

Name	Type	FASTPASS Available	Min. Height	Ages	Description
Kilimanjaro Safaris	Ride	Yes		2+	An open air trip through an African Savannah where giraffes, zebras, lions, and rhinos, and elephants roam
Pangani Forest Exploration Trail	Walk	No		2+	Discover birds, fish, and gorillas in this walking trail
Mickey's Jammin' Jungle Parade	Parade	No		1+	Afternoon parade featuring Disney Characters

Asia

Name	Type	FASTPASS Available	Min. Height	Ages	Description
Expedition Everest	Ride	Yes	44"		Face the Yeti in this rollercoaster thru the unknown
Flights of Wonder	Show	No		2+	Interactive bird show with humor
Kali River Rapids	Ride	Yes	38"		Water Ride—White water rafting experience down the Chakranadi River

| Maharajah Jungle Trek | Walk | No | | 2+ | Discover exotic animals including bats, birds, Komodo dragons, and tigers in this walking trail |

Camp Minnie-Mickey

Name	Type	FASTPASS Available	Min. Height	Ages	Description
Festival of the Lion King	Show	No		2+	Characters from the Lion King sing, dance, and perform the story for guests
Greeting Trails	Meet	No		1+	Meet & Greet with Mickey, Minnie, Donald, and Goofy
Pocahontas and her Forest Friends	Show	No		2+	Children's show featuring Pocahontas and live animals

Dinoland USA

Name	Type	FASTPASS Available	Min. Height	Ages	Description
Boneyard	Play	No		2+	Playground—Dig up bones, and play in the maze built around fossils

DINOSAUR	Ride	Yes	40"		Dark Ride—Go back in time and try to save the last Dinosaur on this thrilling ride. *Can be scary for younger children*
Finding Nemo—The Musical	Show	No		2+	Broadway type, original stage show that brings Finding-Nemo to life right before your eyes through pup-petry and live performances
Fossil Fun Games	Play	No		2+	Carnival style games with a dino twist
Primeval Whirl	Ride	Yes	48"		This spinning coaster sends you through a maze of curves, hills, and drops
TriceraTop Spin	Ride	No		2+	Fly above Dino-land USA aboard a friendly Tricer-atop

Discovery Island

Name	Type	FASTPASS Available	Min. Height	Ages	Description
Discovery Island Trails	Walk	No		2+	Stroll around the Tree of Life and discover animals such as tortoises, lemurs, and tam-arins

| It's Tough to be a Bug | Show | Yes | | 5+ | 3-D show housed inside the Tree of Life featuring Flik and Hopper. *There are parts that can be scary for younger children.* |

Oasis

Name	Type	FASTPASS Available	Min. Height	Ages	Description
Oasis Exhibits	Walk	No		2+	Look for the Giant Anteater, exotic boar, and hyacinth macaw as you walk toward the Tree of Life

Rafiki's Planet Watch

Name	Type	FASTPASS Available	Min. Height	Ages	Description
Affection Section	Play	No		1+	Petting area
Conservation Station	Walk	No		1+	Live animal encounters and interactive exhibits.
Habitat Habit	Walk	No		1+	Discovery trail featuring cotton-tailed tamarins

Wildlife Express Train	Ride	No		1+	Train to Rafiki's Planet Watch which departs from Africa. A one-way trip lasts five to seven minutes.

Epcot: Rides/Attractions/Shows

Futureworld

Name	Type	FASTPASS Available	Min. Height	Ages	Description
Character Connection	Meet	No		1+	Meet & Greet with Mickey, Minnie, Donald, Goofy, Pluto, and Chip & Dale
Ellen's Energy Adventure	Ride	No		3+	Ride with Ellen Degeneres as she travels back in time to the dinosaur era. (45 min)
Honey I Shrunk the Audience	Show	Yes		5+	3-D adventure that features the guests being shrunk and the pitfalls that can occur
Innoventions East & West	Play	No		2+	Various interactive exhibits
Journey into Imagination with Figment	Ride	No		2+	A journey that will engage the imagination and the senses

Living with the Land	Ride	Yes		2+	Boat voyage through amazing greenhouses and a fish farm
Mission Space	Ride	Yes	44"		There are two versions of this mission to Mars: <u>Orange Team:</u> More intense training—*may cause motion sickness* <u>Green Team:</u> Less intense training without the motion simulator spinning
Spaceship Earth	Ride	No		2+	Audio-Animatronic ride through time showing advancements in communication
Soarin'	Ride	Yes	40"		Feel the exhilarating rush of this free-flying hang gliding adventure
Test Track	Ride	Yes	40"		The longest, fastest ride in Disney history. Feel what it is like to travel through a car testing facility
The Seas with Nemo & Friends	Ride	No		1+	Board a "clamobile" & join your undersea pals on a quest to find Nemo

The Circle of Life	Show	No		2+	Short film about conservation with characters from The Lion King
Turtle Talk with Crush	Show	No		2+	Interactive show with Crush the sea turtle

World Showcase

Name	Type	FASTPASS Available	Min. Height	Ages	Description
Gran Fiesta Tour starring the Three Caballeros	Ride	No		2+	Ride along as the Three Caballeros entertain you
Maelstrom	Ride	Yes		5+	Boat voyage through the Viking Era, followed by a five minute movie
O Canada	Show	No		2+	Newly redone Circle-Vision 360 show about Canada (twenty-two minutes)
Reflections of China	Show	No		2+	Circle-Vision 360 film about China. (fourteen minutes)
The American Adventure	Show	No		2+	Inspirational story of America and its people (thirty minutes)

| Illuminations | Show | No | | 2+ | Nighttime fire-works show that takes place on World Showcase Lagoon |

Disney's Hollywood Studios: Rides/Attractions/ Shows

Animation Courtyard

Name	Type	FASTPASS Available	Min. Height	Ages	Description
Playhouse Disney—Live on Stage	Show	No		1+	Live interactive stage show featuring Disney Channel pals
The Magic of Disney Animation	Draw	No		5+	Learn to draw various Disney Characters and see how they are brought to life. There is also a Character Meet & Greet inside.
Voyage of the Little Mermaid	Show	Yes		2+	Live musical featuring Ariel

Echo Lake

Name	Type	FASTPASS Available	Min. Height	Ages	Description
Indiana Jones	Show	Yes		4+	Show featuring edge of your seats stunts

Jedi Training Academy	Show	No		3+	Interactive training experience as you train to be a Jedi
Sounds Dangerous	Show	No		10+	Wacky audio show—*periods of darkness may be scary for younger children*
Star Tours	Ride	Yes	40"		Star Wars flight simulator

Hollywood Boulevard and Sorcerer Hat

Name	Type	FASTPASS Available	Min. Height	Ages	Description
The Great Movie Ride	Ride	No		5+	Travel through classic film scenes and Hollywood moments
High School Musical Pep Rally	Show	No		1+	Join the students of East High in this interactive sing-a-long
Stars & Motor Cars Parade	Parade	No		1+	Afternoon parade featuring Disney characters

Mickey Avenue

Name	Type	FASTPASS Available	Min. Height	Ages	Description
Journey into Narnia	Show	No		2+	Step inside the epic film

The Disney-MGM Backlot Tour	Ride	No		3+	A walking/tram tour of movie making magic
Toy Story Mania	Ride				*Future Ride*
Walt Disney: One Man's Dream	Show	No		3+	A walking tour of Walt's life

Streets of America

Name	Type	FASTPASS Available	Min. Height	Ages	Description
Lights, Motors, Action! Extreme Stunt Show	Show	No		5+	Stunt show that simulates how action shots are made for Hollywood films
Honey I Shrunk the Kids Movie Set Adventure	Play	No		2+	Fun-filled larger than life playground
Muppetvision 3-D	Show	No		2+	3-D show featuring your favorite Muppet characters

Sunset Boulevard

Name	Type	FASTPASS Available	Min. Height	Ages	Description
Beauty & the Beast–Live on Stage	Show	No		2+	Live musical Broadway show (thirty minutes)

Fantasmic!	Show	No		5+	Nighttime spectacular with lasers, lights and dancing water effects. *May be scary at times for younger children*
Rock 'n' Roller-coaster	Ride	Yes	48"		Rollercoaster featuring the music of Aerosmith. Reach 60 MPH in 2.8 seconds!
Twilight Zone Tower of Terror	Ride	Yes	40"		Drop thirteen stories at random times. *May be scary for younger children*

5

Disney Dining

Restaurants

Disney has a variety of dining choices. You have the traditional food court setting, counter service meals, and table service options. There are so many choices for the guests that sometimes there are not enough days in their trip to eat at every restaurant they desire.

You need to know where to start. The first thing you must do if you are traveling during any peak season is to make your ADR's (Advance Dining Reservations). What are ADR's you ask? They are Disney's version of reservations. You can make ADR's for most restaurants 180 days prior to your trip. If you are planning on eating at most of the quality table service restaurants, it is a must to make your ADR's that far ahead. Having ADR's set before you get to Walt Disney World will definitely make your vacation run more smoothly.

How do you make ADR's? At 180 days prior to your trip, you call Disney Dining and request a dining reservation for whatever restaurant you want, give them the date and time. That's it. They will tell you immediately if they have something available. If they do, you will receive a confirmation number and time to arrive. If they do not have anything available you can try another restaurant, or call back in a few days as people may cancel their reservations.

Keep in mind that unlike a tradition reservation, Disney will seat you when the next available table opens for a party your size. Just because you have an ADR for 5:00 PM doesn't mean that you will get seated at 5:00 PM. Most of the time Disney is very good and efficient in getting people to their tables as close to their time as possible. It is strongly advised to show up at least fifteen minutes prior to your ADR time.

The mistake so many people make is thinking that they can walk right up to a restaurant and get a table. During the peak seasons this almost never happens and the look of disbelief on peoples' faces is priceless. Everyone wants to enjoy Disney and the eating choices are bountiful. There are so many unique food samplings to choose from here that planning your dining is almost as fun as planning your vacation. There is something here for everyone in your family.

For dining there are table service (sit down), counter service (walk up and order), and in some resorts, food courts. Some restaurants offer Character Meals, where various characters will come to your table to take pictures with you. Do some research and ask your children which characters they like. That can help you decide which meals they might enjoy. Planning these things many months in advance will alleviate problems when you arrive at Walt Disney World.

Table service meals are traditionally more expensive than the other types of meals. They can range from $15-$125 per person depending on the restaurant you choose. The average price for an adult at a table service runs about $25. These meals usually fill up first during the peak seasons as most guests would like to have nice dinners set up during holiday seasons, especially Christmas Eve and Fourth of July. When you call to make your dining reservations have 2-3 choices in mind, in case you don't originally get what you want. Another good thing to know when making your dining reservations is to go ahead and set up your meals at the 180 day mark from your trip. Even though you may not know which park you will be at 180 days from now, there is no penalty for cancelling a dining reservation. (The exception to this would be a handful of restaurants such as Cinderella's Royal Table & Victoria & Albert's). You will know if there is a penalty by whether or not they charge you ahead of time. Table service dining though does have one negative aspect, time. A table service meal will usually last a family of four at least an hour to an hour and a half. That is valuable touring time in the parks. Many people prefer counter service meals because it's cheaper and quicker.

The next type of dining is counter service. These are cheaper than table service and will range from $5-$15 per person depending on the menu. The average price with a drink is $10 per person. The good part about counter service is that you do not need to make ADR's for them. Another good part is that Disney offers many different menus at their counter service restaurants. Sure some contain the usual burgers and fries, but each park offers several alternative menus. A good idea when eating during peak seasons is to try to eat at non-traditional dining times. Lunch is packed between 11:00 AM and 1:00 PM. For dinner the restaurants are usually full between 5:00 PM and 7:00 PM. Try to avoid this mess, by planning your dining around these times. Eat lunch a half hour earlier than normal or get a late morning snack to tide you over and eat a late lunch at about 2:00 PM. For dinner you can use the same ideas. Eat dinner earlier than normal and snack late at night, or snack in the late afternoon, and eat a later dinner. Anything you can do to avoid dining during peak times will make your life and trip much more manageable. One final reason to eat at a counter service is that it is quick, compared to table service. You can order, eat and be on your way back into the parks in about half the time it would take if you eat at a table service restaurant. This makes for a much better touring plan.

The last type of dining we will talk about is eating at your resort. Most resorts have some sort of food available to purchase. Several have "food courts" or small "grab and go" shops. These can come in handy if you want to eat early before you get to a park. Most are open well into the night so you may find a bedtime treat. Nothing is better than a Mickey ice-cream bar as a midnight snack. The cost of these types of offerings is as cheap or expensive as you want to make it. Most Moderate, Deluxe, and Vacation Club resorts have table service offerings as well.

WDW Peak Season Advice

Do:

- Make your dining reservations as close to the 180 day mark as you can

- Figure out which type of meals your family will enjoy

- Research the internet for menus of various restaurants

- Research the internet so you know the cost of each type of restaurant

- Try to eat at off times if needed (2-3 PM for lunch) to get the restaurant you want if your first time choice is full

- Try another day for the restaurant you want

Don't:

- Make too many ADR's. This can ruin a trip if just as you are enjoying something in the park, you have to leave to go to your dining reservation

- Wait until you get to Walt Disney World to try to make ADR's. You may be very disappointed

Disney's Dining Plan (DDP)

If you book a package with Disney then you are able to add-on Disney's Dining Plan. What is Disney's Dining Plan?

Disney has many signature restaurants as well as its famous Character Dining. The Disney Dining Plan allows guests to choose from over 100 restaurants throughout Walt Disney World. Most of the meals are prepaid in advance, excluding gratuity. Everyone in the room must be on the same package and ticket options.

You will be allocated your meal credits onto each room key. The cost for DDP is $38.99 per adult (ages 10 and up) and $10.99 per child (ages 3-9) per night of stay.

The Dining Plan can be of great savings if you can take advantage of the character meals, as well as the other upscale table service offerings. The downside of the Dining Plan is that you must schedule well ahead. If you are going during any peak season, you must make an ADR at the 180 mark if possible. The restaurants fill up fast and we have seen many people end up disappointed when they walk up and ask for availability and are told there is nothing. The other problem is how will you know what park you will be at 180 days in advance? If you have dinner reservations you then lose some of the spontaneity of your park touring.

Disney even has begun to offer some add-ons to the dining plan such as the *Deluxe Dining Plan*, where you now get the same items as the regular dining plan, plus another snack credit and a refillable resort mug allowing you unlimited non-alcoholic drinks.

Included in the plan are:

- *1 Table Service Meal*

  - buffet & a non-alcoholic drink, OR

  - appetizer, entrée, non-alcoholic drink and desert.

- *1 Counter/Quick Service Meal*

  - one entrée, desert (lunch & dinner) or juice (breakfast), non-alcoholic drink OR

  - one complete combo meal

- *1 Snack—Choice of:*

  - Ice Cream, popsicle, or fruit bar

  - Single serving grab bag of chips

  - One 20 oz. Water, Coke, Diet Coke, or Sprite

- Single piece of fruit
- Medium fountain drink

RESTAURANT KEY:

$= under $10 per person

$$= $10-$20 per person

$$$= $20-$40 per person

$$$$=over $40 per person

B= Breakfast

L= Lunch

D= Dinner

Dining at the Resorts

Each resort has its own dining options ranging from food courts to five-star dining. Listed below are some of the choices available. You can judge what best fits the need of your family.

Value Resorts: Counter Service

Resort	Restaurant	$ and Meal	Comments/Food
Pop Century	Everything Pop	$-B/L/D	Food Court
All-Star Movies	World Premiere	$-B/L/D	Food Court
All-Star Music	Intermission	$-B/L/D	Food Court
All-Star Sports	End Zone	$-B/L/D	Food Court

*There are no Table service offerings for the Value Resorts

Moderate Resorts: Counter Service

Resort	Restaurant	$ and Meal	Comments/Food
Caribbean Beach	Old Port Royale	$-B/L/D	Food Court
Coronado Springs	Pepper Market	$$$-B/L/D	Non-traditional food options
Port Orleans French Quarter	Sassagoula Floatworks & Food Factory	$$-B/L/D	Food Court

Port Orleans River-side	Riverside Mill	$-B/L/D	Food Court

Moderate Resorts: Table Service

Resort	Restaurant	$ and Meal	Comments/Food
Caribbean Beach	Shutters	$$-L/D	American & Caribbean Island entrees
Coronado Springs	Maya Grill	$$$-B/D	American & Mexican Offerings
Port Orleans French Quarter	*No Table Service*		
Port Orleans River-side	Boatwright's	$$-B/D	American food

Deluxe Resorts: Counter Service

Resort	Restaurant	$ and Meal	Comments/Food
Animal Kingdom Lodge	Mara	$$-B/L/D	Food Court & TV for kids
Beach Club	Beaches & Cream To Go	$$-L/D	Burgers & Ice Cream
Boardwalk	Boardwalk Bakery	$$-B/L	Pastries & Sandwiches
Contemporary	Food and Fun Center	$-24 Hours	Snacks & Sandwiches
Grand Floridian	Gasparilla Grill	$$-24 Hours	Snacks & Sandwiches
Old Key West	Good's To Go	$-L/D	Snacks & Sandwiches
Polynesian	Captain Cook's	$$-24 Hours	Snacks & Sandwiches
Saratoga Springs	Artist's Palette	$$-B/L/D	Pizzas/Salads/Sandwiches
Wilderness Lodge	Roaring Fork	$-B/L/D	Snacks & Sandwiches
Yacht Club	*No Counter Service*		

Fort Wilderness	Chuck Wagon	$-L/D	Snacks & Sandwiches
Dolphin	Tubbi's Buffeteria	$-24 Hours	Pizza & Cafeteria
Swan	*No Counter Service*		

Deluxe Resorts: Table Service

Resort	Restaurant	$ & Meal	Comments/Food
Animal Kingdom Lodge	Boma	$$$-B/D	Buffet; Multi-ethnic food offerings
Animal Kingdom Lodge	Jiko	$$$$-D	African dining & cuisine
Beach Club	Cape May Café	$$$-B/D	Character Buffet Breakfast: (Minnie, Goofy, Chip & Dale) & Seafood Buffet Dinner
Beach Club	Beaches & Cream	$$-L	Burgers & Ice Cream
Boardwalk	Big River Grill	$$$-L/D	Burgers & Salads
Boardwalk	ESPN Club	$$-L/D	Burgers/Salads & 100 TV's
Boardwalk	Flying Fish	$$$$-D	Exquisite Seafood Menu
Boardwalk	Spoodles	$$-B/D	Traditional Breakfast offerings & Mediterranean food dinner
Contemporary	California Grill	$$$$-D	Atop the Contemporary Resort one of WDW's finest
Contemporary	Chef Mickey's	$$$-B/D	Character Buffet
Contemporary	Concourse Steakhouse	$$$$-D	Steaks & Salads
Grand Floridian	1900 Park Fare	$$$-B/D	Character Buffet: (Cinderella & Friends)
Grand Floridian	Citricos	$$$$-D	Mediterranean Food

Grand Floridian	Grand Floridian Café	$$-B/L/D	Traditional Breakfast & sandwiches and salads for dinner
Grand Floridian	Narcoossee's	$$$$-D	Seafood Menu
Grand Floridian	Victoria & Albert's	$$$$-D	Disney's Top Formal Restaurant
Old Key West	Olivia's	$$-B/L/D	American Food
Polynesian	Spirit of Aloha Show	$$$$-D	Dinner Show-All-you-can-eat
Polynesian	Kona Café	$$$-B/L/D	American Food with Asian influence
Polynesian	O'hana	$$$-B/D	Character Buffet Breakfast: (Lilo, Stitch, & Mickey) & Buffet Dinner with no characters
Saratoga Springs	Turf Club Grill	$$-L/D	Burgers & Salads
Wilderness Lodge	Artist's Point	$$$$-D	Salmon, Buffalo in a Northwest setting
Wilderness Lodge	Whispering Canyon Café	$$$-B/L/D	Interactive fun; All-you-can-eat meal with barbecue & other meats
Yacht Club	Yacht Club Galley	$$$-B/L/D	Soups & Sandwiches
Yacht Club	Yachtsman Steakhouse	$$$$-D	Traditional Steakhouse
Fort Wilderness	Hoop-Dee-Doo Musical Revue	$$$$-D	Dinner Show with a Western theme. All-you-can-eat meal
Fort Wilderness	Mickey's Backyard BBQ	$$$$-D	Dinner show featuring Mickey & Minnie. Runs March-December weather permitting. Meats & salads are offered.
Fort Wilderness	Trail's End	$$-B/L/D	American food Buffet
Dolphin	Shula's Steakhouse	$$$$-D	Traditional Steakhouse

Dolphin	Todd English's blue-zoo	$$$$-D	Seafood in a modern setting
Swan	Garden Grove	$$$-B/L/D	American Food Buffet
Swan	Gulliver's Grill	$$$-D	Character Buffet Meal
Swan	Palio	$$$-D	Italian Cuisine
Swan	Kimono's	$$-D	Asian fare such as sushi

Downtown Disney Dining: Counter Service

Restaurant	Location	$ & Meal	Comments/Food
Earl of Sandwich	Marketplace	$$-L/D	Fresh-made sand-wiches & Salads
Ghirardelli's Soda & Fountain Shop	Marketplace	$-L/D	Shakes & Ice Cream
McDonalds	Marketplace	$-B/L/D	Standard Menu
Wolfgang Puck's Express	Marketplace	$$-L/D	Fast lunch options such as pizzas
Wetzel's Pretzels	West Side	$-L/D	Pretzels

Downtown Disney Dining: Table Service

Restaurant	Location	$ & Meal	Comments/Food
Bongo's	Westside	$$$-L/D	Cuban inspired menu
Captain Jack's	Marketplace	$$-L/D	Seafood offerings
Fulton's Crab Shack	Marketplace/Pleasure Island	$$$$-L/D	Seafood menu
House of Blues	West Side	$$$-B/L/D	Cajun style and burgers
Planet Hollywood	Pleasure Island	$$$-L/D	Burgers & Salads
Portobello Yacht Club	Marketplace/Pleasure Island	$$$$-L/D	Mediterranean foods & American favorites
Raglan Road	Pleasure Island	$$$-L/D	Irish inspired menu

Rainforest Café	Marketplace	$$$-B/L/D	Sandwiches & Salads
Wolfgang Puck Café	West Side	$$$-L/D	Sit-down dining with a more upscale setting and menu

Dining at the Parks

Each park has its own dining options ranging from on-the-go carts, counter service offerings, or table service meals. A delicious treat awaits you around every corner.

Magic Kingdom: On the Go Carts

Name	Location	$ & Meal	Comments/Food
Aloha Island	Adventureland	$	PINEAPPLE DOLE WHIPS!
Sunshine Tree Terrace	Adventureland	$	Ice Cream, and coffees
Enchanted Grove	Fantasyland	$	Strawberry Swirls & Juices
Mrs. Potts Cupboard	Fantasyland	$	Ice Cream & Shakes
Frontierland Fries	Frontierland	$	McDonalds Fries
Liberty Square Market	Liberty Square	$	Fruits & Snacks
Sleepy Hollow	Liberty Square	$	Funnel Cakes, coffee, caramel corn
Main Street Bake Shop	Main Street U.S.A	$	Cookies, cakes, and pastries
Plaza Ice Cream Parlor	Main Street U.S.A	$	Ice Cream
Toontown Farmers Market	Mickey's Toontown Fair	$	Fruits & Snacks
Scuttle's Landing	Tomorrowland	$	Frozen Cokes

Magic Kingdom: Counter Service

Name	Location	$ & Meal	Comments/Food
El Pirata Y El Perico	Adventureland	$-L/D	Tacos, Nachos; open seasonally
Pinocchio Village Haus	Fantasyland	$-L/D	Pizza, Sandwiches, Soups, Salads
Aunt Polly's Dockside Inn	Frontierland	$-L/D	Snacks; open seasonally
Pecos Bill Tall Tale Inn	Frontierland	$-L/D	Burgers, Sandwiches and Salads
Columbia Harbour House	Liberty Square	$-L/D	Fish and Chicken baskets
Casey's Corner	Main Street U.S.A	$-L/D	Hot Dogs & Fries
Cosmic Ray's	Tomorrowland	$-B/L/D	Burgers, Chicken and Wraps
Tomorrowland Terrace Noodle Station	Tomorrowland	$-L/D	Chicken Teriyaki & Noodle Bowls

Magic Kingdom: Table Service

Name	Location	$ & Meal	Comments/Food
Cinderella's Royal Table	Cinderella Castle	$$$$-B/L/D	Character Breakfast & Lunch(Cinderella & Friends) American Cuisine
Liberty Tree Tavern	Liberty Square	$$-L/D	Character Dinner (Minnie, Goofy &Pluto) American Food
Crystal Palace	Main Street U.S.A.	$$$-B/L/D	Character Meal Buffet (Pooh, Tigger, Piglet, & Eeyore) Standard Buffet menu

The Plaza Restaurant	Main Street U.S.A.	$$-L/D	Sandwiches & Burgers
Tony's Town Square Restaurant	Main Street U.S.A.	$$$-L/D	Pastas & Salads

Animal Kingdom: On the Go Carts

Name	Location	$ & Meal	Comments/Food
Dawa Bar	Africa	$	Snacks & Cocktails
Harambe Fruit Market	Africa	$	Fruits & Snacks
Kusafiri Coffe Shop & Bakery	Africa	$	Pastries & Coffee
Tamu Tamu	Africa	$	Ice Cream
Anandapur Icre Cream Truck	Asia	$	Ice Cream Treats
Camp Soft Serve	Camp Minnie-Mickey	$	Ice Cream
Petrifries	Dinoland USA	$	McDonalds Fries
Safari Coffee	Discovery Island	$	Coffees

Animal Kingdom: Counter Service

Name	Location	$ & Meal	Comments/Food
Tusker House	Africa	$$-L/D	Rotisserie Chicken & Salads
Yak & Yeti	Asia	$$-L/D	Asian inspired
Flame Tree Barbecue	Discovery Island	$$-L/D	Barbecue Ribs, Chicken & Salads
Pizzafari	Discovery Island	$-L/D	Pizza, Salads, Sandwiches

Animal Kingdom: Table Service

Name	Location	$ & Meal	Comments/Food
Rainforest Café	Entrance of Park	$$$-B/L/D	Full service Restaurant with bar
Donald's Safari Breakfast	Tusker House	$$$-B	Character Breakfast Buffet (Donald, Mickey, Minnie, Pluto, Goofy)
Restaurantosaurus	Dinoland USA	$$-L/D	Burgers, Hot Dogs, & Salads

Disney's Hollywood Studios: On the Go

Name	Location	$ & Meal	Comments/Food
Dinosaur Gertie's	Echo Lake	$	Ice Cream Treats
Min & Bill's Dockside Diner	Echo Lake	$	Stuffed Pretzels & Shakes
Peevy's Frozen Concoctions	Echo Lake	$	Frozen Coke
Anaheim Produce Company	Sunset Boulevard	$	Fresh Fruit
Fairfax Fries	Sunset Boulevard	$	McDonalds Fries
Hollywood Scoops	Sunset Boulevard	$	Hand-dipped Ice Cream

Disney's Hollywood Studios: Counter Service

Name	Location	$ & Meal	Comments/Food
ABC Commissary	Commissary Lane	$-B/L/D	Burgers, Fish & Chips
Backlot Express	Near Star Tours	$-L/D	Burgers, Hot Dogs, Salads, Chicken

Flatbread Grill	Streets of America	$-L/D	Sandwiches, salads, and desserts
Toy Story Pizza Planet	Streets of America	$$-L/D	Pizza, Salads, & Arcade games
Catalina Eddie's	Sunset Boulevard	$-L/D	Pizza & Salads
Rosie's All-American Cafe	Sunset Boulevard	$-L/D	Burgers, Chicken Strips, Vegetarian burgers
Starring Rolls	Sunset Boulevard	$-B/L	Pastries & Sandwiches
Toluca Turkey Legs	Sunset Boulevard	$ L/D	Turkey Legs

Disney's Hollywood Studios: Table Service

Name	Location	$ & Meal	Comments/Food
Sci-FI Diner Theatre	Commissary Lane	$$$-L/D	Burgers, Pasta, Seafood
50's Prime Time Café	Echo Lake	$$-L/D	Pot Roast, Meatloaf, Chicken
Hollywood & Vine	Echo Lake	$$$-B	Character Breakfast Buffet (Jo-Jo, Goliath, and Little Einsteins). Traditional Menu
Hollywood & Vine	Echo Lake	$$$-L/D	Traditional Buffet menu
Hollywood Brown Derby	Hollywood Boulevard	$$$-L/D	Steaks, Seafood, Chicken
Mama Melrose Ristorante	Streets of America	$$$-L/D	Italian Cuisine

Epcot: On the Go

Name	Location	$ & Meal	Comments/Food
Epcot Pretzel Carts	Near Mission Space Near Showcase Plaza	$	Pretzels & Drinks
Epcot Espresso Carts	Near Mission Space Near Showcase Plaza	$	Coffees & Pastries
Epcot Snack Carts	Near Mission Space Near Showcase Plaza Near The Land Pavilion	$	Snack, Roasted nuts, & Drinks
Refreshment Port	Near Canada	$	McDonalds nuggets, fries, and drinks

Epcot: Counter Service

Name	Location	$ & Meal	Comments/Food
Electric Umbrella	Innoventions East	$-B/L/D	Burgers, Sandwiches, & Salads
Edy's Ice Cream	Innoventions West	$	Ice Cream Treats
Sunshine Seasons	The Land	$$-B/L/D	Soups, Salads, and Sandwiches
Cantina de San Angel	Mexico Pavilion	$$-L/D	Tacos, Churros, Beer, Margaritas
Kringla Bakeri Og Kafe	Norway Pavilion	$$-L/D	Pastries & Sandwiches
Lotus Blossom Café	China Pavilion	$-L/D	Eggrolls

Sommerfest	Germany Pavilion	$$-L/D	Brats, Pretzels, & Desserts
Liberty Inn	American Adventure	$$-L/D	Burgers, Chicken & Fries
Matsu-No-Ma Lounge	Japan Pavilion	$	Sushi & Cocktails
Yakitori House	Japan Pavilion	$$-L/D	Beef, Chicken, Noodles, Sushi Rolls
Tangierine Café	Morocco Pavilion	$$-L/D	Chicken, Lamb, Sandwiches
Boulangerie Patisserie	France	$	Pastries
Yorkshire County Fish Shop	United Kingdom	$-L/D	Fish & Chips

Epcot: Table Service

Name	Location	$ & Meal	Comments/Food
Garden Grill	The Land	$$$-L/D	Character Meal (Mickey, Chip & Dale)
Coral Reef	The Living Seas	$$$$-D	Seafood & Steaks
San Angel Inn Restaurante	Mexico Pavilion	$$$-L/D	Mexican Cuisine, Margaritas & Beer in a dark romantic setting
Akershus Royal Banquet Hall	Norway	$$$-B/L/D	Princess Storybook Character Dining (Various Disney Princesses)
Nine Dragons	China Pavilion	$$$-L/D	Chinese Cuisine
Biergarten	Germany Pavilion	$$$-L/D	German Meats & Cuisine with live entertainment
Tutto Italia	Italy Pavilion	$$$-L/D	Pastas, Breads, Wines
Teppanyaki Dining	Japan Pavilion	$$$-L/D	Chicken, steak, & Seafood

Tempura Kiku	Japan Pavilion	$$-L,D	Sushi, Seafood, & meats
Restaurant Marrakesh	Morocco Pavilion	$$$-L/D	Beef, Lamb, and Chicken
Bistro de Paris	France Pavilion	$$$-L/D	French Cuisine
Chefs de France	France Pavilion	$$$-L/D	Escargot, Salads, Beef & Wines
Rose & Crown Pub	United Kingdom Pavilion	$$$-L/D	Fish & Chips, Steaks, Beer
Le Cellier Steakhouse	Canada Pavilion	$$$-L/D	Steaks, Pasta & Seafood

6

You've been to the theme parks—Now what?

So you have conquered all four parks—now what? The best part about Walt Disney World is that there is so much to do. The worst thing about Walt Disney World is that there is so much to do. From water parks to fishing to shopping, Disney offers a multitude of activities that can only enhance your vacation experience.

Blizzard Beach

A ski resort in central Florida? It's not what you would expect, but it is what you'll find at Disney's Blizzard Beach. This snowy water park will chill and thrill water slide enthusiasts.

Blizzard Beach's most famous slide is called Summit Plummet, a 120-foot vertical free-falling body slide. It is the tallest water slide in America, and guests can travel upwards of 55 mph as they race to the bottom. From personal experience, I can admit it is rather intimidating to peer over the edge of the slide and see nothing below. I watched helplessly as my daughter was there one minute and POOF-she disappeared down the slide. I had to go through with it once my ten year-old survived the plunge. Get there early because the lines for the chair lift will get long, and it is a very steep climb to the top and an even longer walk back down if you chicken out. Though Summit Plummet is the most recognized of the slides here, there are several other thrill rides/slides such as Downhill Double Dipper, Runoff Rapids, Slush Gusher, Snow Stormers, and Toboggan Racers.

There are tamer slides for your whole family to enjoy together. Teamboat Springs puts you and your family in a raft that will wind down twists and turns to the bottom of the mountain. There is a lazy river for relaxation and even an interactive area for younger children called Tike's Peak. The park also features a main pool area with small waves.

Blizzard Beach truly has something for everyone in the family regardless of age. If you are traveling during the summer, it is advisable to get there at least a half hour before park opening. By 10:00 AM most chairs in the park will be taken.

Typhoon Lagoon

Disney's other water park is Typhoon Lagoon. It is an enormous water park filled with twisting tides, roaring rapids, wonderful waterways and relaxing rivers.

Typhoon Lagoon is famous for its giant wave pool. Every ninety seconds six-foot waves come crashing toward the beach as swimmer try to body surf and float to the shoreline. Beware. The force from these waves can be quite powerful and have been known to sweep kids and adults off their feet. Crush 'n' Gusher is the newest slide at Typhoon Lagoon. It is a raft ride that actually allows you to move uphill similar to a rollercoaster. Typhoon Lagoon also has other water slides such as Gangplank Falls, Humunga Kowabunga, Keelhaul Falls, Mayday Falls, and Storm Slides. The park also has an area specifically for younger children called Ketchakiddee Creek and a lazy river for the family to enjoy. Typhoon Lagoon even offers Shark Reef, a saltwater snorkeling adventure with real sharks and schools of colorful tropical fish.

One note to consider is that since Typhoon Lagoon is older, it does not have some of the modern features of Blizzard Beach. At Typhoon Lagoon you will have to drag your raft up many flights of stairs before you ride. Blizzard Beach has a mechanical conveyor belt system to transport your rafts up the hill for you for most slides. After hauling those huge rafts up numerous flights of stairs you will hear that lazy river calling your name for sure.

Recreation

Disney also offers some other recreation type activities for guests in case they want an alternative to visiting a theme park. The following is a list of some of the best activities for those who want something to do instead of a theme park visit.

Bike Rentals

Wheel around Walt Disney World in a relaxing setting with your entire family. The following are locations that offer bike rentals:

* *Disney's Boardwalk Inn Resort*

* *Disney's Caribbean Beach Resort*

- *Disney's Coronado Springs Resort*
- *Disney's Fort Wilderness Campground*
- *Disney's Old Key West*
- *Disney's Port Orleans French Quarter & Riverside Resorts*
- *Disney's Saratoga Springs Resort*
- *Disney's Wilderness Lodge Resort*

Fishing Excursions

Cast your line and reel in the fun on a two-hour fishing excursion on the lakes of Walt Disney World. For reservations please call 407-939-2277. The following are locations that offer fishing excursions:

- *Disney's Boardwalk Inn Resort*
- *Disney's Caribbean Beach Resort*
- *Disney's Contemporary Resort*
- *Disney's Coronado Springs Resort*
- *Disney's Fort Wilderness Campground*
- *Disney's Grand Floridian Resort*
- *Disney's Old Key West*
- *Disney's Polynesian Resort*
- *Disney's Port Orleans Riverside Resort*
- *Disney's Saratoga Springs Resort*
- *Disney's Wilderness Lodge Resort*
- *Disney's Yacht Club*
- *Downtown Disney Marketplace*

Golf Courses

Disney is also home to championship and award winning golf courses. There are six golf courses available and each offers a different skill level and quality. For golf tee times please call 407-938-4653, or you can book tee times on-line through the Disney World website. The following are a listing of choices:

- *Lake Buena Vista*

- *Magnolia*

- *Oak Trail*

- *Osprey Ridge*

- *Palm*

Kids Programs

Walt Disney World offers many excellent kids programs. Treat your child to one of the magical Disney kid programs and know that they will be supervised by a trained professional staff. Some of the kids programs are listed below:

- **Children's Activity Centers**—For ages 4-12 who are toilet trained, Disney's Children's Activity Centers feature computer & Arcade games, arts & crafts, movies and dinner and snacks.
  - *Disney's Animal Kingdom Lodge Resort*
  - *Disney's Beach Club Resort*
  - *Disney's Grand Floridian Resort*
  - *Disney's Polynesian Resort*
  - *Disney's Wilderness Lodge Resort*

- ***Disney's Grand Floridian Resort*** is home to these kid activities (ages 4-10) For reservations call 407-WDW-DINE
  - Grand Adventures in Cooking—children will make cookies
  - Wonderland Tea Party—Have tea with Alice and the Mad Hatter
  - Disney's Pirate Adventure—set sail and discover hidden treasures

- **Kids Nite Out**

  - Treat yourself to a night out while your child gets one-on-one childcare in the comfort of your hotel room. For reservations call 407-828-0920

Marina Watercraft Rentals

Captain your own adventure as you sail across various waterways on the Walt Disney World Property. You can rent a Sea-Ray boat, a sailboat, or a pontoon boat, as well as other watercraft like kayaks, canoes, or pedal boats. The following are locations that offer these rentals:

- *Disney's Beach Club Resort*

- *Disney's Caribbean Beach Resort*

- *Disney's Contemporary Resort*

- *Disney's Coronado Springs Resort*

- *Disney's Fort Wilderness Campground*

- *Disney's Grand Floridian Resort*

- *Disney's Old Key West*

- *Disney's Polynesian Resort*

- *Disney's Port Orleans Riverside Resort*

- *Disney's Wilderness Lodge Resort*

- *Disney's Yacht Club*

- *Downtown Disney Marketplace*

Miniature Golf

Walt Disney World offers you the chance to relax and play at its two fantasy courses. Each is beautifully themed and offers a different experience.

- *Disney's Fantasia Gardens Miniature Golf Course*—themed after the Classic Disney Movie Fantasia

- *Disney's Winter Summerland Miniature Golf Course*—located next to Disney's Blizzard Beach Water Park, the ski theme has transformed its way to this course as well.

Resort Spas

Everyone likes to be pampered and why not on your trip to Disney. Disney offers two major spas while they also have six limited service spas.
<u>Full-Service Spas:</u>

- *Grand Floridian Spa* (call 407-824-2332 for reservations)

- *The Spa at Disney's Saratoga Springs Resort* (call 407-827-4455 for reservations)

<u>Limited-Service Spas:</u>

- *Disney's Animal Kingdom Lodge*

- *Disney's Boardwalk Inn*

- *Disney's Contemporary Resort*

- *Disney's Coronado Springs Resort*

- *Disney's Wilderness Lodge*

- *Disney's Yacht Club Resort*

Richard Petty Driving Experience

Who hasn't wanted to be able to drive a NASCAR racecar? Well, at Walt Disney World you can get the behind the wheel and take it for a spin around the track. Located at the entrance to the Magic Kingdom parking lot, a NASCAR race team will train guests who to experience this thrill. For reservations call 1-800-237-3889

Water sports

Disney offers some of the best water sport activities around. The Seven Seas Lagoon in front of the Magic Kingdom provides the setting for these exhilarating experiences. To book any of these adventures stop by the Sammy Duvall's Water Sports Centre located at *Disney's Contemporary Resort Marina*. You can also book on-line at <u>www.sammyduvall.com</u> or by calling 407-939-0754.

- Waterskiing

- Parasailing

- Wakeboarding

- Tubing

- Personal Watercraft

Wide World of Sports Complex

This is a sports facility with basketball, football, softball, and baseball fields together in one place. It hosts various youth and adult tournaments throughout the year. The Pop Warner Football Championships are held annually in early December. The complex is home to the NFL's Tampa Bay Buccaneers Training Camp in July. During March it becomes home to Major League Baseball's Atlanta Braves for their Spring Training. In 2007 it even played host to regular season baseball games for the Tampa Bay Devil Rays.

Walt Disney World also provides two other areas for entertainment, *Downtown Disney* and *Disney's Boardwalk*. Each area offers guests a relaxing and exciting escape from the hustle and bustle of a day at the parks. There are restaurants at both locations, which were described in Chapter Five, as well as shopping and nightly entertainment.

Downtown Disney

Downtown Disney is an area that has been developed into a shopping, restaurant, and nightclub district. It is divided into three unique sections: The *Marketplace, Pleasure Island,* and *the West Side.* We have already discussed the restaurants in Chapter Five, so let's look at what else is offered.

Marketplace

Name	Comments
Marina & Boat Rental	Rent a variety of boats and travel on the waterways from Downtown Disney to Old Key West, Port Orleans, or Saratoga Springs Resorts

Goofy's Candy Company	Interactive fun and loads of candy offerings
Disney Tails	Disney themed souvenirs for your pet
Mickey's Mart	Disney character merchandise under $10
Pooh Corner	Everything a Pooh fan would want in one store
Disney's Days of Christmas	Year Round holiday gifts
Disney's Wonderful World of Memories	Photo albums, stationary, picture frames, and scrapbooking
The Art of Disney	Disney fine art gallery
Mickey's Pantry	An assortment of Disney home and kitchen products
Once Upon a Toy	Classic games and toys with a Disney twist
Disney's Pin Traders	Largest Pin trading station at Walt Disney World
Summer Sands	Fun in the sun swimwear and casual clothing
Team Mickey	Tons of sports items, including ESPN themed merchandise
Arribas Brothers	Crystal, collectible, engraving and artist's demonstrations
Basin	Unique bath and facial products
Bibbidi Bobbidi Boutique	Where little girls feel like Disney Princesses. Hair styling, make-up, nail polish, or princess packages are available. Reservations are strongly encouraged by calling 407-939-7895
World of Disney	The ultimate Disney interactive shopping experience. Largest Disney shop on property
Lego Imagination Center	Every Lego toy imaginable is here

Pleasure Island

Name	Comments
Sosa Family Cigars	Premium smoke shop
Orlando Harley-Davidson	Genuine T-shirts, gifts, and collectibles. See custom Harleys on display
Motion	Nightclub featuring Top 40 Music with a live DJ

Rock 'n' Roll Beach Club	Nightclub featuring live rock and DJ
Mannequins	Nightclub featuring revolving dance floor
8TRAX	Nightclub featuring music from the 70's and 80's
Comedy Warehouse	Improv comedy show
Adventurers Club	Explore rooms of zany explorers recalling outrageous adventures
BET Sound Stage	Nightclub featuring Hip=Hop and R & B music

West Side

Name	Comments
Cirque du Soleil—La Nouba	Mesmerizing experience with daring acts of physical artistry and imagination. For tickets call 407-939-1298
Disney Quest	Five floors of interactive games and rides
Disney Quest Emporium	A cool collection of Disney gifts
AMC Pleasure Island	24 movie theatres
Virgin Megastore	A music, movie and multi-media extravaganza
Pop Gallery	Enjoy a glass of Champagne at this colorful art and gift store
Magic Masters	Spellbinding gifts and magic demonstrations
Hoypoloi	Contemporary three dimensional art shop
Sunglass Icon	Sunglass fashions from around the world
Disney's Candy Cauldron	Scrumptious sweets in a show kitchen
Magnetron	Magnet shop
Planet Hollywood on Location	Planet Hollywood gift shop
Starabilias	Nostalgic celebrity memorabilia
Mickey's Groove	Disney Character Merchandise

Disney's Boardwalk

Disney's Boardwalk is an area that has been developed into a shopping, restaurant, and nightclub district, like Downtown Disney only on a smaller scale. We have already discussed the restaurants in Chapter Five, so let's look at what else is offered at the Boardwalk.

Disney's Boardwalk

Name	Comments
Wyland Galleries	A classic gallery of marine life featuring the internationally renowned artist
Thimbles & Threads	Ladies, children, and infant apparel plus Disney Character merchandise
The Yard	ESPN Merchandise
The Yard Arcade	Try your hand at various video games in this arcade
Screen Door General Store	Snacks, beverages, and Disney merchandise
Pin Station	Official Disney Pins sold here
Dundy's Sundries	Boardwalk logo merchandise, gifts, sundries, and film processing
Disney's Character Carnival	Adult and Golf apparel, accessories, and Disney merchandise
Atlantic Dance Hall	Nightclub featuring Dance Music, and also plays host to Disney Vacation Club's *Welcome Home Wednesdays* for members.
Jellyrolls	Dueling Piano and sing-a-along bar
Midway Games and More	Test your skills at basketball, bell ringing and more
Performers on the Boardwalk	Nightly at various locations, performers such as magicians will appear and offer interactive tricks for their audiences.
Surrey Bike Rental	Try a trip around the lake on a bike built for two, four, or eight people

Disney Extras

We all know that any vacation to Walt Disney World is a big financial invest-
ment and many times people focus on how much it costs to do things. However,
one of the best features of Walt Disney World is that it offers so many cheap or
free things to do in and out of the parks.

Our first suggestion is to visit the other resorts. Each resort offers a different
theme or setting than the others. Many of the resorts offer table service restaurants, which are fun to eat at because they may offer a unique menu vs. some of
the restaurants in the parks. Each resort also offers different merchandise as well.
The Christmas season is the one time of year that you should try to visit as many
resorts as you can. Again visiting resorts is free, and Disney will provide transportation to and from each park to every resort for you. From early December until
early January every resort and park dons its holiday decorations. Many of the
resorts offer holiday activities for the kids as well as carolers or live music. Again
most of these activities are free. Some resorts even have cookies and lemonade
available for their guests.

Another idea for an activity outside the parks is to purchase an arcade card for
your child. This isn't the cheapest thing to do, but if you purchase a $25 card it
allows your child hours of time playing games. The cards can be used at any
resort so if you are resort hopping, be sure to bring it along. In our experience the
Value resorts offer the best bang for your buck in regards to the game selection.

Pin trading is an activity that guests of all ages can enjoy. Cast members will
happily trade Disney pins with you as you work your way through the parks.
This can be a bit addictive and expensive. Sometimes the quest to get that certain
Mickey pin has resulted in forgetting about a ride or show.

Inside the parks, believe it or not, there are some cheaper options that you
might overlook. Each park and many rides have "Hidden Mickey's" (a large circle
with two smaller ones located above the large circle to form Mickey Mouse's head
and ears). These are great for you or your children to look for all over the parks.
They are everywhere, but of course many are "hidden". Again, this is a fun activity that is free. Another activity inside the parks is to just take in all the details in
every ride, store or sign you see. The difference between Walt Disney World and
other parks is that the Imagineers have tried to create a story for everything they
do in the park. Every ride has a back-story, as do the shows, shops, and even the
queue lines. Take some time and look up at the ceilings or at the posts you see.
For example, read the hilarious signs as you make your way through the Jungle
Cruise queue line. Listen carefully to background music as well. Spend your

Expedition Everest wait time examining the artifacts brought back from the Himalayas. Many times there are Imagineering gems there that most people won't even pay attention to because they are focused on the ride itself.

You can also visit characters inside the parks. There are meet-n-greets all over. Look on the park maps for locations for various characters. These are the perfect opportunity for you to interact and get photos as well as autographs with some of your favorite characters. Some of your most special Disney memories may come from these character moments.

In my opinion, one of the best free things to do though is to ride on the monorail. Even if the monorail isn't going to your eventual destination, ride it around for a bit. If you have the time, ask one of the Cast Members at the monorail station if you can ride in the front car of the monorail with the driver. You may have to wait for the next monorail to arrive, but this is something that kids will remember for their entire lives.

The final cheap activity is to just enjoy your own resort. Take some time to walk around it. Check out the architecture and the unique features it offers. Take a swim in the pool. Ask about Hidden Mickey's around the resort. Appreciate the details that went into the design. These quiet times can be overlooked as guests are so excited about trying to take in everything else at Walt Disney World. Sometimes exploring and enjoying your resort is a relaxing (and free) thing to do.

WDW Peak Season Advice

Do:

- Visit other resorts

- Ride the monorail, especially the front if you can

- Look for Hidden Mickey's everywhere

- Find things your kids will like that are free such as the dance parties

- Visit the Boardwalk area in the evening

- Get photos with the characters throughout the parks

- Enjoy your own resort. You picked it for a reason

Don't:

- Think you have to just spend money to have an enjoyable trip
- Ignore the little things throughout the parks

Afterword

My wife, two daughters, and I are lucky enough to travel to Walt Disney World three times a year (albeit during the three Peak Seasons). Sure enough every time we talk about where we are going for vacation we continually get asked, "You're going to Walt Disney World again? Why?" To us it is funny because other people will go to their favorite beach or timeshare every year at the same time and that is ok. These people ask us how we can possibly go to Walt Disney World again and again. These are the people who just don't "get" Disney and never will. Too bad for them that they can't enjoy the magic that Walt Disney World offers.

So, why do we keep going to Walt Disney World? That is simple. It is a safe place where adults and kids can both have a great time. The Walt Disney World resort area is 47 sq. miles so there is plenty to do. Anyone who has been inside the Walt Disney World boundaries and has had to leave the property for some reason can understand the difference. What is it? I am not sure how to describe it. There is just a feeling you get that while you are inside the Walt Disney World property you are in a protected environment, away from the rest of the world. Right after you leave the Walt Disney World property you are instantly back to the reality of traffic, commotion, and in general, the hectic daily life you were trying to avoid for a few days. Walt Disney World has created the perfect setting for children and adults to bond together, to relax, and to have a great time. To that extent Walt Disney World was created in the way Walt truly imagined. The one thing that I think really makes people understand what Walt Disney World offers is the look in the eyes of children when they see a resort, or a park, or a character for the first time. When you see the excitement on their face, most people "get it." Others may "get it" when they go to the park as an adult, yet can still feel like a kid again as they fly with an elephant or climb into a teacup. Some people "get it" when they put on those Mickey ears or find themselves hugging a duck. Put away that cell phone, stop texting the office, and let yourself be immersed in the magic.

Whatever is in the pixie dust, it has enchanting qualities that can wash away your troubles while you wish upon that star. That is why we go to Disney again and again and again … even in the peak seasons.

Please let us know your thoughts

- Tell us what you liked about <u>Walt Disney World Peak Seasons: Maximizing your Disney Vacation</u>.

- Tell us how we can improve the next edition

- Share with us your stories about vacationing during any peak season.

- Do you have any tips that you use to maximize your Disney vacation during a peak season?

You can let us know at our website: <u>http://www.wdwpeakseasons.com</u> and clicking on the email link.

Walt Disney World continues to change and evolve every year. Things such as park hours, events, prices, policies, shows and attractions will change. This book has given you as accurate information as possible. In order to get up-to-date information such as park hours, discount codes, the latest Disney news, and other Disney information please stop by our website.

The website was designed and created for you. It was created in response to so many Disney websites that are difficult to navigate. This site is user friendly giving you what you need to know in a simple format. Please visit us, give us your feedback, and most of all, enjoy.

Index

978-0-595-47727-2
0-595-47727-5

Breinigsville, PA USA
27 November 2009
228254BV00002B/1/A